LEADERSHIP SAVVY

WHAT TO DO AND WHAT **NOT** TO DO
TO BE A **STAND OUT** LEADER

**10 Most Common Leadership Mistakes
10 Management Myths
5 Keys to Career Success**

Nikki Hanna

Published by Patina Publishing
727 S. Norfolk Avenue
Tulsa, Oklahoma 74120
neqhanna@sbcglobal.net
www.nikkihanna.com

Copyright © 2011 by Nikki Hanna

IBSN 978-0-9828726-1-1

CONTENTS

INTRODUCTION

I. 10 MOST COMMON LEADERSHIP MISTAKES

1. Not Realizing the Significance of **Integrity**
2. Not Understanding the **Scope of Leadership**
3. Underestimating the **Breadth of Accountability**
4. Lack of **Courage**
5. Overlooking the **Value of Diverse Talent**
6. Adopting a **Victim Mentality**
7. Not Recognizing a Leader's **Role as Nurturer**
8. Too Much Focus on **The Job You Want**
9. Failure to Articulate the **Purpose of Work**
10. Undervaluing the **People Component**

II. 10 MANAGEMENT MYTHS

1. Anything Worth Doing is Worth Doing Well
2. Always Be Fair
3. Protect Your Staff from Adversity

Contents

4. Always Defend Your Employees
5. Conflict is Inevitable
6. Employees Dislike Work Measurement
7. If You Work Faster, You Make More Mistakes
8. To Resolve Issues, You Must Find the Truth
9. Getting Ahead Is All About Who You Know
10. The Enforcers Are Out to Get You

III. 5 KEYS TO CAREER SUCCESS

1. Aspiration
2. Endurance
3. The "And Then Some"
4. A Learning Environment
5. Expertise

SUMMARY - THE SAVVY LEADER

APPENDIX
Sample: **Core Values**
Sample: **Behavioral Model**

INDEX OF BEST PRACTICES

ABOUT THE AUTHOR

TO ORDER

INTRODUCTION

Leadership can be defined in many ways. It is often associated with words like directing, controlling, and governing. Most people view leadership as having power and influence. All these attributes fall under the leadership umbrella, but they don't really get to the intrinsic nature of it and the immense and generous prospects it offers.

> The essence of leadership suggests opportunity, a chance to have an impact, to matter in a profound and positive way. The fundamental key to realizing this constructive interpretation of leadership is to embrace it from the perspective of *service*--making a difference for those you lead and those you follow.

Work gets done through people. Accomplishments happen because people make them happen. Not much really happens individually when you think about it. Even your personal achievements involve many other people.

Becoming a *savvy leader* requires a deep interpretation of leadership. When viewing leadership through the lens of service to others, you are postured to ensure that those around you are successful and therefore in a position to

Introduction

champion your own achievements. This perspective also provides an avenue through which you, as a primary player, shape your company as a prosperous industry leader--one that invests in the people who make success happen.

Viewing leadership as service to others and behaving within that context influences behavior in a way that will differentiate you--allow you to STAND OUT from the pack through a rare and powerful awareness. By steering ambition in a positive direction, this perspective fosters an environment where you leave your mark all over an organization in constructive and remarkable ways.

There are several sound reasons for striving to be an extraordinary leader, one being your personal sense of accomplishment. Another is doing something meaningful. The most vivid rationale, though, is interpreted from a practical standpoint. There are only so many leadership positions available in an organization and considerable competition for them. If you want one, you must have an *edge*. You have to STAND OUT for all the right reasons. To do so, there are things you need to know, things you need to do, and things you should **not** do.

> **TEN LEADERSHIP MISTAKES:** It has been suggested that inspiring leadership through listing mistakes, as is done in this book, takes on a negative tone. However, a savvy leader is never afraid to face negatives head on. Although anyone can appreciate focusing on good behavior, it is difficult to conceive of rectifying unfortunate behavior by ignoring it. Consequently, this book boldly confronts behavior that doesn't work well for an aspiring leader.

Introduction

There are plenty of rousing cheerleading books out there on leadership focused primarily on what to do. This one does more than that. Cutting to the chase--the mistakes--this narrative tells you what **not** to do.

TEN MANAGEMENT MYTHS: These myths are generally accepted in many quarters, even in the business community. Almost always they are applied in ways that hamper positive outcomes and limit career options.

Although these pre-conceived notions are dispelled here, many are deeply engrained in our culture and some readers may disagree with the suggestion that they are, in fact, myths. Admittedly, some have validity on some level and in certain situations, but the *savvy leader* will interpret them with rational thought and apply them with astute, discriminating judgment in the business setting.

FIVE KEYS TO CAREER SUCCESS: These points simplify and clarify many of the nuances of realizing ambitious aspirations. An abundance of information is economically condensed into five concise and manageable categories focused on setting the aspiring leader apart from the pack.

Few people make it to the highest ranks of an organization. Those that do must STAND OUT in an impressive manner in order to compete successfully for the limited slots. These five keys to success articulate how to do that.

Introduction

If you aspire to be an exceptional leader, to advance your career, to climb the corporate ladder or whatever other achievement you seek, you will find the information in this book invaluable. An abundance of books have been written on leadership. This one focuses on fresh insights, practical applications, unique perspectives, and proven strategies targeted at providing you, the aspiring leader, with innovative approaches that will set you apart, give you an edge, and make you a *savvy leader*.

More importantly, though, is the prospect that through leadership you will find a way to "matter," to put your stamp on an organization, and to make a difference for others through *service*.

10 MOST COMMON LEADERSHIP MISTAKES

LEADERSHIP MISTAKE - 1

Not Realizing the Significance of INTEGRITY

Success doesn't count if you don't have integrity. In fact, nothing counts if you don't have integrity.

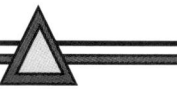

Most people underestimate integrity's role in their life. Integrity is everything to a leader. If you don't have that, nothing else matters.

Integrity has been defined as doing the right thing, being honest and forthright, and behaving in an ethical manner. All of these descriptions fall under the integrity umbrella and certainly can drive good behavior, but integrity is really much deeper than that. It goes to the core of who you are as reflected in what you do minute-by-minute every day. **Integrity is everything**. It is:

- Telling a clerk she gave you too much change
- Keeping confidences
- Showing respect for others, no matter their status
- Good manners
- Being on time

- Doing what you say you will do
- Showing up
- Being real and forthright
- Admitting when you are wrong
- Not leaving your trash in the airline seat pocket
- Every action, minute-by-minute, day-by-day

When is an action so small that it doesn't count? Never.

THE POWER OF INTEGRITY: There is incredible power in being a person of integrity. It empowers an individual more than any other redeeming quality they might cultivate and produces character, confidence, a strong sense of self, and inner strength. It defines who you are. Integrity can be your anchor, an internal compass with which to navigate the maze of life's decisions and actions.

Becoming a person of integrity is a continuous process, and no one ever really reaches the point of absolute integrity or perfection. We are all human and therefore flawed, but aspiring to be a person of utmost integrity and functioning daily with an awareness of that is crucial to winning the respect, hearts and minds of others and thereby becoming a STAND OUT leader.

INTEGRITY GAPS

An expedient path on the journey toward integrity is to look for situations where your words do not match your actions. These are "integrity gaps." Get rid of them. Stop saying it or stop doing it. Never say one thing and do another.

Employees will spot *integrity gaps* with amazing proficiency. To them it is a blatant betrayal when you say one thing and do another. It is the quickest path to disrespect you will ever experience. One of your most valuable assets in the work environment is *employee loyalty,* and it goes out the window with your lack of credibility. Don't say it if you can't back it up.

> Anything you require of your followers you need to do yourself. If you promote a strong work ethic, you better have one. If you expect people to be at work on time, you better be there before them. If you demand compliance, and you should, don't pad your expense report. If you want your people to care about the customer, you must demonstrate that you care about the customer.

Integrity is not something you have, it is something you do, and you do it whether anyone is looking or not. Because everyone is constantly bombarded with integrity challenges, acting with integrity requires sacrifice, dedication, and constant vigilance. Since it is a reflection of who you are, and you cannot effectively lead without it, an intense focus on self-monitoring of behavior is a worthy endeavor.

Your integrity is about every aspect of your life. Behaving differently at work than in your personal life signals an *integrity gap.* With a solid sense of self, you will establish a standard of behaving in the world that is beyond reproach in all settings. Compartmentalizing your life produces inner conflict. Be who you are all the time and everywhere. Make that something of which you can be proud.

Becoming aware of *integrity gaps* puts an individual in a position to eliminate them. Doing so inspires a positive sense of self and a profound source of inner strength. People will follow that. They will want what you have.

CORE VALUES: Defining a set of core values can be invaluable in influencing integrity. As a leader you can create a framework for employee behavior by defining a set of *core values* for your company or department that are clearly communicated to employees as a requirement for employment.

> **CORE VALUES**
>
> **An approach to discovering your personal integrity base is to articulate core values through words that describe how you live. They provide a framework for everyday living and a basis for making decisions on how to behave. On a deeper level, they define who you are. The same is true for an organization, and articulating those values in a *core values statement* ensures that all employees are aware of the company perspective.** (See Appendix for a sample Core Values Statement)

A *core values statement* can express what your organization is about through such words as respect, encouragement, honor, duty, accountability, collaboration, integrity, and service. Words can clarify how your company defines integrity. As all employees internalize the meanings of the words, *employee loyalty* and cohesiveness blossom. Everyone is operating from the same frame of reference.

The approach to developing core values is critical.

- Seek employee participation in establishing them.
- Define each value.

- Tie each value to specific behaviors that reflect that value.
- Constantly communicate and reinforce those values, orienting all new employees on them.
- Include evaluation of core value behaviors in performance appraisals.
- Continuously reinforce core values in training materials and communications.
- Require conformance, responding quickly to any noncompliances.

Over time, the investment in identifying and championing core values has a powerful positive influence on employees and the organization. Additionally, embracing values at work fosters personal growth and is, therefore, a gift to the people who work for you.

BEHAVIORAL MODEL

Once core values are articulated as a list of words that describe what your organization is about, a *behavioral model* can clarify behaviors required to reflect those values. This tool communicates with clarity to everyone in the organization how they are required to act in the work environment. (See Appendix for a sample Behavioral Model)

Because of the ingrained nature of behaviors, it is important to orient everyone when rolling out a core values statement and a behavioral model. Employees need to know how to challenge non-compliant behavior in a non-threatening way. Conversely, when challenged, they must learn to respond positively.

> An email from a company leader included an instruction that was contrary to the company's core values. Interestingly, the only person who called him on it was a new supervisor who responded with an email stating he was confused by the instruction which was in conflict with the company's values. He was right, and he had the gumption to call an executive on it. The leader revised the email, and in it he thanked the employee profusely for having the courage to point out his lapse. It was a matter of integrity on both their parts to do what they did.

People act the way they do because it worked for them in the past. Depending on your company, introducing core values may require a substantial shift in corporate culture. Your leadership through this process is vital. **Remember, it is what you do, not what you say that counts most.**

Behavior is a choice. Core values and *behavioral models* are tools that drive constructive perspectives and positive behavior by providing a framework for making decisions and choosing how to act. Your company may not have formally established core values, but a savvy leader will have them in his areas of responsibility. By setting the tone and creating the environment in which people function, he sets the integrity bar.

Don't make the mistake of ignoring the role integrity plays in your ability to be an effective leader. It supports *employee loyalty* and promotes inner strength, confidence, and self-respect. If you are to be successful, you will want that for yourself and everyone around you. Integrity is a gift to others. Sharing it is a generous way of *serving* those you lead.

LEADERSHIP MISTAKE - 2

Not Understanding the SCOPE OF LEADERSHIP

Everybody leads.
Everybody.

Everyone sees their management team as leaders, assuming it is the title and position that make them so. The truth is, every person in an organization is a leader. Everyone has some level of influence. Not grasping this concept and the power it generates results in lost opportunities to tap into a prolific human resource available to a leader.

EVERYBODY LEADS

Leadership is the ability to influences others. Everyone does that, all day every day. You do not have to be in a formal position of authority to lead. EVERYBODY LEADS.

Little babies lead. If you don't believe that, just try to ignore one when he is hungry. All of your employees play a leadership role. Everyone is always leading. **A person**

cannot NOT lead. An extraordinary leader recognizes that and takes advantage of it. Since few leaders do this, it can set you apart. If you can ultimately inspire all the leaders in your organization to embrace this concept, it can set your company apart from the competition.

The most lucrative source of leadership in most organizations is not recognized or utilized.

PEER LEADERSHIP

There are positive and negative forces in the employee ranks and both are leading. The positive forces are those employees who diligently do their job every day. They work hard, roll with the flow, remain positive, and quietly maintain their focus no matter what--staying the course in times of turmoil. Consequently, they are often ignored while the negative forces of trouble makers and drama seekers get most of the attention from the organization's leaders. A savvy leader empowers positive employees as *peer leaders* and disempowers negative forces.

As you gain insight into the value of these steady workers as leaders, it becomes obvious that enhancing their influence can have a significant impact on other employees. What if everyone thought and acted like them? What if the voices of these employees were as loud as those of employees who overreact and view everything negatively?

A formal program to increase the influence of positive *peer leaders* was introduced in a company. Steady, loyal, committed employees were identified and designated as ambassadors for employees and advisors to management. Trained on communication skills, they became valuable credible messengers.

An annual recognition program provided acknowledgements and commendations for their contributions, and each year new employees were rotated into the ambassador role. This incentivized other employees to aspire to be a part of this group, and the peer leader program became a powerful positive influence.

This program proved especially important in the process of acclimating new employees. When joining a work group, new people had historically been highly influenced by the more vocal employees. Certainly any militant employee is going to latch on to the new blood. By assigning each new employee to a peer leader buddy, positive relationships were encouraged and *employee loyalty* enhanced.

Don't make the mistake of underestimating the capability of every employee to influence no matter what their rank or function. A savvy leader recognizes that EVERYBODY LEADS and taps into the potential of empowering positive influences and minimizing negative ones.

LEADERSHIP MISTAKE - 3

Underestimating the BREADTH OF ACCOUNTABILITY

You are, in one way or another, accountable for everything.

If you are late to a meeting, you may use the excuse that traffic was bad. However, one could make the point that you should have accounted for that when you decided when to leave for the appointment. If you had allowed time for bad traffic and left sooner, you would have been on time. Consequences may not be intended, but they are always to some extent the result of a decision and action on your part.

An extraordinary leader applies accountability broadly, both to himself and others. When unfortunate things happen, he sees it this way: **Reasons and excuses may be interesting, but they don't change anything.**

By stopping at reasons and excuses, you are not being accountable. There has to be action. **First you've got to fix the bad outcome, and then you must fix the process that allowed it to happen.** This means you do whatever needs to be done to prevent it from happening again. In other words, you must actually DO SOMETHING.

DO SOMETHING MANAGEMENT

If something is wrong, regardless of the reasons and excuses, own it, fix it, be all over it. DO SOMETHING. This includes taking steps to ensure the incident never happens again.

PREVENTION: This last step in dealing with a problem is crucial and requires getting to the root cause of the incident--not the explanation or excuse, not the symptom. **Don't confuse symptoms with root causes**.

A critical requirement of prevention is solid root cause analysis. If you trace back far enough, you will find that the root cause is always some action for which someone is accountable, and it might not be the most obvious person.

> In a committee meeting an unfortunate incident was explained at great length and in substantial detail by a department head. The report even named the person to blame for the fiasco, a lower level employee who executed the action. There was no mention of any management responsibility for the lack of policies and procedures that would have prevented the incident or any proposed action to install them. Reasons and excuses were made, an employee identified to blame, and that was it.
>
> That was the first mistake. The second one occurred when the committee accepted the report. Under this circumstance, odds are this incident or a similar one **will** happen again. Needless to say, morale among the troops working for this leader, who was focused on reasons, excuses and blame, was low. Further,

the entire employee base was most likely plagued with repetitive problems because their leaders did not take problems to the level of corrective action.

Always put the emphasis on actions to correct and prevent. When you serve on a group that is receiving a report, don't accept one that does not include correction and prevention. A savvy leader assumes responsibility and requires that of others. This includes in-depth root cause analysis and preventative action.

> An employee was fired for going four hundred thousand dollars over budget procuring a system. Certainly he was "held accountable," but where was his boss? How did the employee spend all that money without anyone knowing it? Were there no project status reports, budget reviews or internal controls required? Had no one communicated requirements to the employee up front?

There is no defense for what the employee did, but there is also no defense for what management did **not** do. There is no real accountability in a scenario where a lower level employee is blamed for something and leadership simply explains it. **Root causes are often a lack of adequate procedures, checkpoints, and management oversight.**

OUTCOMES AND PROCESSES: Full accountability means taking ownership of all *outcome*s whether good or bad, as well as any *processes* and *methods* used to produce them. Requiring routine reporting is a valuable tool to ensure that individuals are held accountable throughout the process of delivering outcomes.

DIRECT REPORTS MUST REPORT

Regular reporting mechanisms are a must for any leader. They can be a formal written report, a staff meeting, a project update, or an informal Friday afternoon email. Whatever form they take, you must require that your staff report to you routinely so you know the status of their activities. This allows you to hold them accountable for the processes as well as the end results of their activities.

Conversely, if you are an effective leader and a good communicator, you will report on a frequent and regular basis to your boss, WHETHER HE REQUIRES IT OR NOT. In addition to you being accountable, this provides an opportunity to inform your boss in a humble, matter-of-fact way of the impressive things you are doing. He may not know if you don't tell him.

RESCUES: Take a deeper look at situations where people are always rescuing. Are they really heros?

> A manager was frequently considered a hero for his valiant efforts to bring inventories down to an acceptable level. However, no one thought to consider why they were repeatedly rising to unacceptable levels in the first place. A root cause analysis revealed that introducing practices to better manage the work force and to make processes more efficient could stabilize inventory levels.

Accountability

Situations where constant rescuing is happening are rich targets for a savvy leader to STAND OUT. Frequently everyone is congratulating the hero. You, on the other hand, are seeking root causes and solutions to prevent the problem in the future so the rescue is no longer necessary. Your leadership will model the process of applying penetrating analysis to problems which will make everyone in your organization more effective.

TRYING: Take this word out of your vocabulary. Trying doesn't cut it. There is no accountability in trying. Results are what count. You either do it or you don't. Although giving something a good effort is commendable, it doesn't deliver. You do a whole bunch of valiant trying with no results, and you've got nothing. A savvy leader never says "I'm trying," and his employees don't say it either.

DEPENDENCIES: Dependence on others may impact an outcome in your area, but you are still accountable for it. If people are not supporting you, DO SOMETHING.

> A company had a provision in its contracts that was extremely difficult to administer. Employees just couldn't seem to get it right. Manual processes were so complex that outcomes were plagued with errors, and the team was unable to get the ultimate fix of automation from an under-resourced systems department. Finally they sought a solution through the product development and legal divisions by getting the provision removed from the contract--a brilliant out-of-the-box solution that eliminated any dependencies.

Simply reporting a problem and using the excuse that another department is not supporting you produces no results. You must fix it. This means you or your staff may have to lead a work group that should technically be lead by another department. Whatever it takes, hold yourself accountable for what your area delivers and be all over it.

When unsuccessful at getting a solution, don't accept failure. Document and broadly publish the problem emphasizing the impact on customers, employees, and costs. Use this information to engage other stakeholders and anyone else who can influence resolution. Conduct brainstorming sessions. **There is always a solution. Pursue a resolution relentlessly until you find it.**

Naive leaders are quick to assume they are not responsible for certain outcomes because they believe they are beyond their control. This is an unfortunate perspective the savvy leader avoids. He knows he is accountable for everything.

LOW MORALE?
THE PROBLEM IS YOU.

If you have low morale in your area of responsibility, YOU are the problem. The level of morale among employees is the result of leadership, or lack of it. The buck stops with you.

An effective leader realizes he creates the work environment. A study of military history reveals that in the most adverse situations imaginable leaders have inspired their troops in astonishing ways and kept morale high. Since your situation does not in any way approach that level of challenge, the prospect of you leading your troops through adversity with confidence and enthusiasm is high.

If you look at root causes of low morale, you will find problems with you or your management team's actions that cause it. When one of your staff tells you morale is low, hold him personally accountable for that and assist him in discovering what he is or is not doing to influence the environment.

HIGH TURNOVER?
THE PROBLEM IS YOU.

You can always find plenty of excuses for high turnover, but people rarely leave a job because of pay, benefits or promises from other companies. They leave because of their leaders. If they feel appreciated, valued, and supported, they are loyal and don't even look for another job.

A poor performer leaving is *positive turnover*. (You should explore why they were hired in the first place.) Another form of *positive turnover* is when an employee is promoted. An effective leader coaches and grooms employees for promotions and celebrates when they get them, even if they go to another department. On the other hand, turnover of good employees for other reasons signals a problem for which you are accountable, and you need to DO SOMETHING.

> It is important to note that when there is high turnover, the people leaving are the good employees. They can leave. They have opportunities and they know it. The work unit is then left with marginal employees who will stay no matter what. Their options are limited. Over time, this significantly degrades the work force and when sharp people are hired, they don't feel like they fit in. Hot shots want to work with other hot shots. They want to be proud of their work and their team, and they will go where that is achievable.

High turnover reflects a lack of *employee loyalty*, a serious and costly problem requiring immediate and aggressive action on your part.

To retain a loyal base of steady strong performers, you need to know why good people are leaving. **Most reasons people give for quitting a job are not the real ones.** In-depth, independent exit interviews provide valuable information on the real reasons for turnover.

Whatever is causing people to leave, the leadership in that area is accountable for it. If solid, long-term employees are abandoning ship, especially for lateral positions, you've got a serious, costly problem you need to get all over.

> A manager with high turnover in her area explained the problem this way: People were leaving because of a company policy allowing lateral transfers and a grading system which attracted employees to another area with higher grades. She said these were corporate policy issues over which she had no control. These were **REASONS** and **EXCUSES,** and she stopped there. The fact that she did that reveals the real **ROOT CAUSE** of the problem--her leadership.
>
> The manager's boss held her accountable and required further research into the cause of the problem. An employee survey revealed a management style that resulted in a negative environment which was driving turnover, particularly the lateral transfers. That and the manager's lack of initiative in seeking solutions and challenging policies that negatively impacted her area were the ROOT CAUSES of the high turnover.

In other words, it was lack of leadership and accountability.

With this information, a three-part action plan was put into place. First, a personalized leadership development plan was implemented for the manager. Second, she collaborated with human resources to stratify grades within the department thereby creating career paths. Third, she asked for a review of the incompatibility of grades throughout the company which resulted in some positions in the department being upgraded. That was **ACTION** and **PREVENTION**.

It was a full court press, and it worked. The problem shifted from the explanation and excuse mode into the action mode where root causes were identified and targeted action taken to prevent turnover. This was accomplished because the manager was held accountable for the problem and was required to DO SOMETHING beyond explaining it. She became a better leader as a result. No matter what else is going on, turnover is almost always a leadership issue.

A company experienced a peak in turnover because a new company moved into town and was hiring its best people away with higher salaries. Management reacted, insisting on a survey of area salaries which resulted in an increase in the pay scale. Leaders also educated employees on their benefits, which were better than the competitor's, and introduced more flexible work hours. Because managers were empathetic and understanding when employees left, they were eventually able to recruit some of the better ones back by offering to bridge their years of service. When things shook out, the turnover subsided, and the competitor was left with the less stellar employees.

It would have been easy for management to simply explain the turnover. Certainly they had a good reason for it. Instead, they took accountability for the outcome and approached the problem from the perspective of **own it, fix it, be all over it. DO SOMETHING.**

DO SOMETHING, EVEN IF IT'S WRONG

In some instances it is best to do something, even if it is wrong. At first blush this sounds like a scary proposition, but it is often better to act and possibly make a mistake than to ignore a problem and do nothing. Under the do nothing scenario, you have a guaranteed bad outcome. Under the do something scenario, you at least have a crack at a positive one.

As a leader, be cautious about being hard on employees who take actions that don't turn out well. They could have played it safe and done nothing. You want employees with the courage to take risks, respond to problems and DO SOMETHING.

WE'VE ALWAYS DONE IT THIS WAY: If you are a leader, you already know this is no excuse for anything, but do all you employees know it? Don't accept this mentality from anyone. It reflects a blatant ignorance of accountability, and guess who is accountable for that--the leader of the person who said it. If you hear this from anyone in your area, you have some serious training to do.

Accountability

YOU TOLD ME TO DO IT THAT WAY: Another way an employee will often avoid accountability is to meticulously follow instructions even if things are not going well.

BLIND HERD MENTALITY
When an employee is delivering bad outcomes and does not report the problem or do anything to fix it, he is demonstrating blind herd mentality. He justifies this by maintaining that a policy or someone of authority told him to do it that way, suspending all individual thought, judgment, and accountability.

Employees new to management are particularly vulnerable to this. Create awareness among all of your employees of their obligation to fix problems if they can, and if not to report them vigorously. Anytime employees or customers are experiencing negative outcomes, action is mandated. Employees should never ignore such a situation. They should **own it, fix it, be all over it. DO SOMETHING**.

MASS PUNISHMENT: It is important that the consequences for accountability are applied to the right people.

MASS PUNISHMENT
Naive leaders will punish a whole department for the bad behavior of a few. This is extremely de-moralizing to those not involved in the behavior. Direct any actions designed to hold people accountable to the people that are, in fact, accountable.

If one employee does not comply with requirements, don't tighten the policy for everyone. Narrow the scope of the punishment to the specific person or persons involved. In most cases, you may want to take advantage of the opportunity to give a lesson of what not to do to everyone, but don't punish them.

Require that all employees have a DO SOMETHING mentality, especially your management team. Without full accountability they cannot be strong, capable leaders. **When there is mediocrity in your management team, there will be mediocrity in your operations.** Excellence will not be achievable, and employees, customers, and the company cannot reap the rewards of being winners. Set the bar high for your leaders and for yourself. Teach them to be accountable, to be DO SOMETHING managers.

Savvy leaders apply accountability broadly. There are always solutions. If there is a problem, they are going to Own it, fix it, be all over it. They DO SOMETHING.

LEADERSHIP MISTAKE - 4

Lack of COURAGE

*You want to be a leader, you've got to "buck up."
If not you, who?*

The easiest thing to do is nothing. Fear freezes. It takes *courage* to be a risk taker, to buck up and face whatever challenge is presented and deal with it head on.

> A young supervisor volunteered to take on a problem that was controversial and politically sensitive. He was told by another supervisor that he was a fool for doing so. Guess who saved the day on a critical project with his intervention, and guess which of the two supervisors the boss promoted the first chance he got.

A savvy leader will put everything on the line. At the same time, he has a sense of balancing the risks of doing so with potential consequences--a matter of judgement. He has the patience to wait for the right moment and knows it may be necessary to go to the well many times to make something happen, but when the moment is right, he seizes it. **Putting it all on the line when your gut and your logic tell you it**

Courage

is the right thing to do and the right time to do it, well, there is just nothing else like it.

With integrity and accountability mastered and an understanding of the scope of leadership, you are postured to lead with courage and panache and doing so will set you apart. Visible opportunities to do this are bountiful. For example:

> Whether the reasons are valid or not, the unfortunate mob behavior of verbal bashing often emerges in meetings. This is not appropriate in the business setting. Be the stand up person who brings the group back to rational discussion and the mission at hand. This is a visible "seize the moment" opportunity. Take it. Be the rational voice of logic. If not you, who?

THE COURAGE TO FIND YOUR STYLE: In the mist of a distinct corporate structure, you can find your own style. It is best not to get too "out there" and make a right turn down crazy street, but done right finding your own personal style can turn you loose and light you up.

> A woman found her stride in a company when she realized that trying to match the corporate behavior of others was simply not working for her. At one point she believed she had climbed as far as she could up the corporate ladder and had nothing to lose, so she decided to take a risk and be more true to herself. She found her own style.
>
> In meetings, the executives were cool, calm and collected, unless they were attacking each other for sport. Although the sport was entertaining, it was not her natural mode of operation, and she was not

really a cool, calm and collected kind of gal. She was a rather high energy, action-oriented person, and she started acting that way. She went a mile a minute. When she made presentations she talked fast and over-sold her ideas with passion. She was not "cool." She was a raving activist.

Instead of following the pattern of delivering surprise rebuttals in meetings for sport, she went to people ahead of time, told them she was going to disagree with their proposal, and then gave them the reasons so they could prepare to counter her objections. This was viewed by others as weakness. She didn't care. She wasn't in it for sport.

Things were getting done and long-running problems were being resolved. In spite of her blatant enthusiasm, which she had feared would be irritating to the cool and collected crowd, her behavior was tolerated with good humor. To her amazement, she was promoted. It was hard to argue with the unprecedented results generated from all that energy.

You will never be extraordinary if you don't find your style. Just remember: **Everything involved in becoming successful is a matter of balance. You can do too much or too little of anything.** Walking the line requires an intuitive feel for how far to go, when to go, and when to pull back--all a matter of judgement. Be a *prudent risk taker*. In finding your style and turning it loose, consider the corporate culture in which you are operating. Ignoring it completely or adhering to it too strictly both have a price.

IMAGE: You may be surprised to realize this topic falls under the category of *courage*, but it does take a degree of audacity to do this right, primarily because you will most likely have to buck the trend. If you look serious and professional at work, other employees with a different agenda may try to derail you.

> A young man always wore dress pants, dress shirts, sports coats and loafers to work in an office environment where he was not required to do so. A coworker who dressed for farming said to him one day, "Who are you trying to impress?" The young man answered "Well, not you, that's for sure." Today he is an executive.

Not every work environment requires a professional appearance, but whatever the situation, look at how the people dress who will be promoting you and take your cues from them. It may seem like a trite subject, but how you dress for work is an extremely lucrative and often overlooked career opportunity.

DRESSING STUPID

> **Aspiring leaders do many difficult things and make a lot of sacrifices to get ahead. They dedicate themselves to their company, pursue degrees and credentials, and work long, hard hours. Then, with one simple decision, many of them jeopardize it all. They dress stupid.**

> **On the other hand, with no monetary investment or effort, they can do something every morning that sets them apart and has a significant positive impact on their career. They don't dress stupid.**

One reason this is so important is that many people do dress stupid. Most companies of any size have a dress code, and many people look for every occasion they can find to violate it or at least take issue with it. Not doing so and simply following the code affords you an incredible opportunity to set yourself apart, to demonstrate that you are "with the program." It is important to note, however, that you can follow the code and still not dress properly.

> An executive created an opportunity for one of his hot shot employees to make a presentation to a board. The employee dressed so bizarrely that it was quite a distraction, and the officer took considerable ribbing as a result. He felt betrayed. The employee's redeeming qualities were negated by poor judgment on what to wear to work that day.

If you have no interest in getting ahead, knock yourself out. Dress stupid and challenge the dress code. If you want a career, here is what you do:

> Everyone has the right clothes in their closet. Make the decision every day to wear them. Dress according to code--always--no exceptions.

> If your company has no dress code, dress like the people who are going to promote you.

> Put your work clothes in a separate place in your closet and only wear those to work.

> When tempted to wear something non-compliant, ask yourself, "Do you want a promotion or not?" If so, do what you need to do to get it.

Courage

On jean days don't dress so poorly that if someone tossed you a rifle, you are ready to go hunting, or handed you a pitchfork and you are all set to put up hay. Most employees fail to consider that you don't "have to" wear jeans on jean day, but if you do, buck the trend and take it up a bit.

You are competing with others for promotions. It is not likely you will be promoted just because you dress the part. There must be substance behind the look, but you sure don't want to **not** get promoted because of appearance. Your image can make a difference. You didn't do all that work to get ahead just to sabotage yourself with how you look. If you do, anyone with good sense would question your judgement.

You are creating your "brand" by your appearance. Consider what you want that to be. **It is impossible to make a neutral impression with how you look, and your look tells the world how you feel about yourself.** It sends a message. Send one that says you are serious--that you are a leader. You might be able to get ahead no matter how you dress, but if that dress is non-compliant with a code or out of step with those making decisions, odds are against it.

FIRING: Nothing puts the fear into anyone more than having to fire a poor performer, but you must muster the *courage* to act when circumstances dictate.

Why let an employee go? Why not just accommodate the non-performer? If you are a savvy leader, you will build an exceptional team. Although it is easy to coast along and accept poor performance, and it seems expedient to tailor a job down to someone's limited capabilities, both are a betrayal of the employees who do perform, your customers, and yourself. Additionally, not addressing performance issues threatens the respect of employees, peers, and superiors. It is also incredibly expensive. The waste is huge.

- Calculate the cost per year of a D performing employee contrasted with an A performer.
- Multiply this cost times 30 years.
- Add to that the cost of 30 years of reduced production from all other employee who are not going to work as hard as they can because you do not require it of the D employee.
- Calculate the cost of re-work and doing the work the D employee does not get done.
- Add to this management's time spent dealing with the poor performer and smoothing things over with others.
- Consider how much business is lost over a thirty-year period because of increased prices and sub-quality products or services from a poor performer.
- Multiply this cost by the number of D's in your department.

The cost is astronomical, almost beyond comprehension, and you have not even considered the costs of any F's in your operation. Deal with employees who can't or won't perform. Turn a D or F position into an A. You can't afford not to. The performance gap between the two is enormous.

Employees are paid and receive benefits for doing a job. They need to do it. Most people who are not performing know it and don't feel good about it. For others, though, part of their incompetence is their inability to recognize their own incompetencies. Under either of these scenarios, people are not happy, but they hang on.

> A low performing employee had been trained three times. As she was being terminated, she maintained she was not adequately trained. The manager pointed to fifty other employees in the work area and with a clear conscience told her, "These people have been trained once and are doing the job. We are not training you again."

Many performance problems are behavioral. Keep in mind that **behavior is a choice.** Make certain your employees know this. **The ball is in the employee's court to meet requirements, to behave responsibly and in concert with the company's core values. The ball is in your court to require they do so**.

When you are getting complaints about an employee from other employees and customers, investigate thoroughly and document. Never ignore them. When you have coached, supported, trained and re-trained, and the employee does not perform, you have the basis to let him go. With performance measurements and documented requirements consistently applied to all employees, performance below minimum standards is cause for termination. Make certain no one is performing below the level of the employee you are letting go.

Include performance requirements in job descriptions and appraisals. **Don't wait for scheduled appraisal times to act. React as soon as you observe any performance or behavioral inadequacies. Never save up performance issues for the appraisal process. There should be no surprises during an appraisal.**

If you inherit long-term employees who have never performed, and no one has dealt with that, give them support. They may perform once they know it is required. If they don't, you have to act. Just because they have been there a long time does not mean they are there forever.

Repeated core value violations require termination, no matter how strong the performance.

> The strongest performer in a department was disruptive. Getting her work done quickly, she spent time causing trouble. The manager finally let her go. Employees were so glad that they made up the difference. Her disruption was equivalent to one person, and it was not necessary to fill the vacancy.

Involve the legal and human resource areas of your company and your boss at the first sign an employee is not viable. Become an expert on requirements for terminations. Don't over-invest in time and effort to counsel and de-hire. The requirements are clear, and you've given the employee plenty of support. They either meet them or they don't. Counseling sessions should be short and to the point. Documentation does not mean lengthy write-ups. They can be simple bullet-point accounts of performance as compared to requirements, short notes on counseling and training sessions, and routine appraisals. Long, drawn out write ups are not required.

When letting someone go, treat the person respectfully. Remain unemotional, calm and matter of fact. An employee might react irrationally, you cannot. Show empathy. It is a sad situation when someone loses a job. It is also sad when other hard-working employees incur the ramifications of someone not carrying their weight and getting paid for it.

COMPASSION: If your organization is not for profit, you may have different standards for holding employees to performance requirements, although it is unlikely it is prudent to ever sacrifice behavioral standards.

If your company is for profit and competing in a free market environment, you have a fiduciary responsibility to run your department with sound business and economic principles. On the other hand, you have a moral obligation to be charitable. Nurturing deserving employees in a state of crisis and hiring those with disabilities or special limitations is another way you can dedicate your leadership to *service*. There is a time and a place for this and legal and human resources associates can provide counsel on how to do so without jeopardizing holding employees to standards of performance.

PROMOTING: If done right, promoting people requires *courage*. There are pressures and distracting influences around the selection process, and the decision probably has more impact than you realize.

THE MESSAGE

Every time you promote an employee, you send a clear and resounding message to the rest of the staff about what you value and what it takes to get ahead. This is a rare and profound opportunity. Don't waste it. Consider *the message* when making a promotion decision.

When you promote someone who politicked or lobbied for their position and didn't really earn it, you send a disheartening message to those who have done what should be done to get the promotion, and it rarely works out well in the end. The person did not pay their dues and was simply not ready. What he has proven is that he is good at politicking, and that skill may not have any relationship to the work being done.

When promoting, **don't confuse likability with competence.** This is not a personality contest. You are looking to make the best match of talent to the work. **Select the candidate with the innate skills for the job. You can give someone the knowledge and information to do it, you cannot give them inherent capabilities.**

A common promotion mistake is promoting based on performance at the current level. **Don't confuse technical ability with leadership ability.** There is a different skill set for leading than for doing the work. A few people have an aptitude for both, most do not. It is tempting to promote the strongest technical performer into management, but you make that mis-step and everyone loses, the exceptional employee you promoted most of all. Odds are he will eventually be in your office begging you to get him out of the situation, that is if he doesn't just out-and-out quit. Have the *courage* to do the right thing.

HIRING: Installing people matched to the work takes considerable finesse and often the *courage* to buck up to your own boss who is not as close to the operation as you are and may have a different agenda. Step up and make your case with vigor on who to hire. You may also have to challenge legal and employment department policies. Many companies are cautious about using pre-employment screening tools. If you are going to hire well, you need them.

> A department had a 40% failure rate of new hires. The work was detailed, demanding, highly technical and required a rare combination of skills which were not obvious in a job interview. Some positions

turned over twice in a year. A pre-employment screening program was introduced that ensured people hired had the appropriate skills. The first forty people hired under this process trained up quicker, performed better, and stayed longer than the historical average resulting in an incredible 0% failure rate.

It is mean to hire a person into a position for which they are not well suited. It sets them up for failure, and you are not going to deliver the excellence to which you aspire. Additionally, the effort expended in hiring and training is wasted, and you have to start over with another person who also has a high probability of failure.

Hire well. Train your staff on interviewing and selection techniques. Seek processes and tools to screen employees effectively and match applicants to the work to be done.

Include the company's employment office and legal staff when exploring pre-employment screening options. Use expert consultants to validate them to ensure applicability and reduce legal risks. **In reality, any legal risk from someone screened out for a job up front is probably significantly less than the risks associated with the numerous and complicated processes of dealing with a mis-hire.**

It is important to make certain screening processes are appropriate and properly applied. The objective is to match people to work, not to discriminate on any other level.

OPERATIONAL ISSUES: It requires *courage* to confront policies that don't work, fight for resources, and demand needed support from ancillary areas, all things a leader typically must do. Most likely every leader will occasionally have to confront the difficult tasks of cutting costs and carrying out lay offs. **Challenging times require extraordinary actions.**

Many leaders become upset to the point of distraction at having to make deep cost cuts or lay people off. A savvy leader will face an operational crisis with *courage* and use it as an opportunity to do things he might ordinarily not be able to do. He will execute a full court press, become more proficient, go after waste with a vengeance, seek efficiencies from every angle, discriminately cut costs, lay off the lowest performers and inspire those remaining to do more with less. As a result, his team will become leaner, meaner and stronger. He will not lead them down the victim path. He will go for the win.

TOO MANY WHELMS: You may be confronted with projects or promotions for which you feel you are not ready. Every accomplished leader has had the experience of feeling he is in over his head. Unless your gut tells you it is a career path that absolutely will not work for you, have the *courage* to take it on. Someone had confidence in you or they wouldn't have asked you to do it. If you find the challenge an overwhelming prospect, look around at who else is doing it. If they can do it, you can. **You get an opportunity, you take it. If you are not ready for it, get ready. Dig in, learn, and just do it.**

THE COURAGE TO WAVER: For some reason, people often perceive changing your mind as negative--a weakness. They label it "wavering." However, if you gain information that indicates a position you have taken needs adjustment, have the *courage* to change your mind. If people want to call that "wavering" and attach a negative connotation to it, that's their deal. You are a rational, logical thinker. **Don't apologize for changing your mind.**

Having the *courage* to take risks and "buck up" are required if you expect to deliver exceptional results. When others don't step up, you do. Doing so is reflective of your view of leadership as *service*, which inspires you to act--to make a difference. You have faced the question, "If not you, who?" and you know without a doubt, it is you.

LEADERSHIP MISTAKE - 5

Overlooking the VALUE OF DIVERSE TALENT

*It's a good thing we are not all just alike.
Our differences are what make us strong as a team.*

There is a natural tendency to gather people around you who think and act like you, but doing so is a huge mistake. A savvy leader surrounds himself with people with common core values but divergent talents and varied perspectives. It is a good thing we are not all just alike, and diversity is the key to successful, effective teams. People who are different can counter-balance team weaknesses as well as your own and ensure better decisions and results.

If you are not strong in organization and administration, you need someone on your team who is. If you are not a technical wizard, you need one. Whatever your weak points, seek out team members and leadership staff who are strong in those areas.

It is interesting to note that in an organization with many functionally diverse departments, those departments will take on distinct personalities. Employees with certain characteristics cluster into professions compatible with their character traits, skills, and aptitudes. This is why you see "marketing types" in marketing and "technical types" in the technology area. People clearly gravitate to professions based on their innate abilities.

To optimally utilize human resources, it is important to match people to the work they will be doing. However, everything is a matter of balance. If you load a department full of people who are alike, they may perform that area's basic function well but make uninformed decisions and have difficulty interacting with other departments that have a different personality and perspective. They are also unlikely to reflect their diverse customer base.

> A director over a technical area did such a good job of matching job applicants to the work that over a period of time his department was loaded with talented technical experts but devoid of anyone with leadership skills. Not only did his staff not have the aptitude for it, they had no interest in it. He had no manager or project leader prospects.

This is an example of how you can do too much or too little of anything. Finding balance is a key imperative for building a strong team. What is the answer to the dilemma of hiring people with certain aptitudes for the work while at the same time cultivating a diverse employee base? Here are some things you can do.

- Seek out people with the skills you need who have another complement of innate qualities. Look for the technology person with leadership skills and the marketing one with administrative ability. They are somewhat rare, but they are out there.

Diverse Talent

- Teach your leaders to value the "characters" in their departments, the people who are different. There is a tendency to consider them odd or weird rather than just different. Listen to them and relish their unique qualities. Since people gravitate to groups where they feel comfortable, you must make a special effort to hold on to them.

- Look for ways to integrate diverse functions into the work area that attract people with a different skill set. Add project management, coordination, quality control, technology, testing, documentation or training.

- If you are fortunate to have people in your area who want to remember people's birthdays, decorate for holidays, and bake cookies to make everything better when times are tough, embrace that. They are not normally attracted to the business environment. You need them.

- Be open to other perspectives. People who are different from you don't expect you to always agree with their opinions or adopt their ideas, but they need to know they are heard, that you are appreciative of their creative participation. Welcome fresh ideas, encourage out-of-the box suggestions, and embrace innovative solutions.

PILOT PROGRAMS

When wrestling with whether to do something proposed by someone whose views are very different from yours, let them test it out in a pilot program. This is a controlled risk situation, and you

> **might be surprised how many times these ideas work out. If not, the damage is contained, you all learned something, and employees know you take them seriously and value their creative ideas.**

PREJUDICE: Everyone knows you cannot tolerate prejudices in the workplace, but if you are a savvy leader, you will take this to another level. Lead your team beyond tolerance to valuing diversity. It is the key to a strong team and provides an opportunity to *serve,* to make the work environment better for all. It also allows you to create a team representative of your customer base.

We have all been exposed to prejudices, often not based on personal experience but on what we were taught.

> A midwestern farm woman, who was never exposed to diverse people in her environment, was taken on a vacation to Hawaii where she declared, "This place is full of foreigners." It was quite a shock to her when she was told she was the foreigner.

We are all foreigners somewhere. Every single person is different. We all have diverse backgrounds, unique experiences, and our own way of viewing the world. These differences are what make each of us special and give us value. They are also the basis of a strong team.

You will have prejudiced employees on your staff. This is your chance as an extraordinary leader--to enlighten and influence. Beyond the act of making it clear that prejudicial behavior violates the core value of respect and will not be tolerated, you can paint a picture of the value of differences and thereby orchestrate progress. Your behavior alone will speak volumes.

Working together on projects is an excellent way for diverse people to learn to share information and thereby begin to value each other. Put together diverse work groups. Incorporate themed lunches and holiday celebrations into the company social calendar. Through sharing, employees will discover a common humanity. Bottom line, with very few exceptions, all people want the same thing--their families to be safe and to prosper.

GENERATION GAPS: An emerging social issue seeping into the workplace is related to generation gaps which are said to be wider now than at any time in history. As a leader you can influence employees of every generation to value each other and learn from each other. Don't allow any generation to be dismissive of the other. Every generation brings something to the table. A department composed of all age groups is rich in character and more likely to be representative of your customer demographics.

TEAM BUILDING: Work gets done through people. The most important thing you will do in your job is build your team. No matter what attributes you personally bring to the table as a leader, if you cannot put together a *smokin' team*, you cannot deliver exceptional results and you will not be a STAND OUT leader.

One of your biggest challenges will be to get divergent employees to work together effectively. Because various personality types perceive the world differently, they are going to respond in unique ways to situations in the workgroup process. It is helpful for team members to understand how and why each personality type responds differently to the same stimuli. With this awareness, they will interpret team members' behavior more appropriately.

> Employees in a company were interpreting the behavior of those in another department as persecution. They believed the staff purposefully set out each day to treat them badly. A personality assessment program took the mystery out of the behavior. Understanding triggers for negative behavior, employees realized their own actions were threatening, thereby driving the bad behavior. None of it was conspired or intended, but simply a natural defensive response of that personality type to a perceived challenge.

Employees learning the dynamics around the diverse perspectives of various personality types experience personal growth that influences both their professional and personal lives. There are a number of programs that create awareness of the basic personality types, how each views the world, and how they naturally behave. Seek one out and enlighten your employees. **Keep in mind that people choose their behavior and being a certain personality type is never an excuse for bad behavior, and that all types are good. None is better than the other, they are just different.**

An added bonus to enlightenment on these divergent personality types is that they are also representative of your customer population. An awareness of the natural behavioral patters of various personalities will make employees more effective and responsive when accommodating customers and selling to them.

Another bonus of the awareness of personality types and how they behave is a personal one. With this knowledge, employees' personal relationships are enriched because they more astutely interpret behavior of their spouses, in-laws, children and others.

EXPONENTIAL SYNERGY: It is challenging to find a more powerful combination of words than *exponential synergy*.

> **Exponential** refers to an increase that is becoming more rapid. **Synergy** is when the combined effort of a group of people working together as a team is greater than the sum of all their individual efforts.

By removing barriers and championing employee learning, you increase the rate of progress of people and projects, and the *exponential* effect kicks in. By putting employees together into powerful teams that deliver something greater than employees could do individually, *synergy* is generated.

Doing all of these things (removing barriers, championing employee learning, and creating powerful teams), releases the expansive power of *exponential synergy*.

PROGRESS SQUARED

> **Let's say you have a staff of six managers and, in addition to their daily operational duties, you assign each a project. You remove barriers to their efforts and train them on project leadership, teamwork, and how to tap into *diverse talent*. As a result, all six are more effective and generate increasingly more rapid results. Progress is *exponential*. Then you put them together in project teams, and the magic of *synergy* happens. The result of your investment in these managers will reflect powerful and lucrative *exponential synergy*.**

That is not all. As six leaders and their diverse teams learn from this process. They can now apply their newfound knowledge to the next project, and the next, and the next. You are going to turn them loose again and again, and each time they are more seasoned. Each time more *exponential synergy* kicks in and more magic happens.

There is more. What these managers learn trickles down to their employees, which means approximately three hundred people are going to deliver more rapid results and more effectively participate on teams. This is *progress squared*.

Realizing *progress squared* is dependent on strong, diverse teams. A savvy leader is a champion of diversity and an expert at team building. He takes advantage of whatever unique talent each employee possesses. He teaches his employees that everyone is different, that diversity is universal, and it is a good thing. The savvy leader is just as likely to celebrate the fact that someone is from Montana as he is to celebrate the Chinese New Year. There is so much to celebrate about people, and he makes certain everyone knows it.

Value the individuality and uniqueness of every person and encourage other employees to do the same. Celebrate differences, match people to work that complements their talents, encourage their learning, team them up, remove barriers and watch the *exponential synergy* kick in. Reap the benefits of *progress squared*.

LEADERSHIP MISTAKE - 6

Adopting a VICTIM MENTALITY

Play the cards you are dealt and go for the WIN. When you go down the victim path, you LOSE and you take everyone else with you.

Everyone wants to be a winner, but people will sprint down the victim path so fast it will make your head spin. As an influential leader, you can take them there in a heartbeat. Don't do it. Make your team winners, not victims.

WINNERS vs VICTIMS

The tendency to embrace victimization in our society is cultural. Our legal system, media, political environment and a host of other components encourage the victim mentality. One of the most effective ways to manipulate people is to convince them they are being victimized. Don't do it. A savvy leader does not want a team of victims. He wants winners.

Victims operate from a perspective of being persecuted which promotes a host of unfortunate behaviors. To avoid

Victims vs Winners

this, a savvy leader will inspire his team to win. He wants capable, strong, solution-oriented people who insist on **winning--no matter what challenges are presented**, people who are focused on embracing reality and courageously **playing the cards they are dealt.**

It is easy to fall victim to influential people in your organization who are running their own personal agendas. You depend on them to get your job done, but they don't deliver. Others want to support you but, for whatever reasons, they cannot. Do not use their lack of support as an excuse for poor outcomes. **Look for ways to reduce dependencies and focus on what you can control. It is up to you as the leader to ensure that the job gets done no matter what. Don't be a victim. Find a way to win.**

> A customer service operation had a severely inadequate system and a technical staff that did not have the resources to support it. Consequently, the service staff slipped into the victim mentality. They complained a lot, struggled with the daily work processes, and invested considerable time and effort begging for help and developing proposals that never got approved or funded. Sadly, they had an excuse for not delivering the service levels they knew their customers deserved, so they felt defeated. THEY WERE LOSERS.
>
> Finally, their leaders decided to stop investing time and effort into trying to get support and instead set about focusing on what they could control. They developed manual processes to offset system inadequacies. Although this appeared at first blush to be a tremendous step backward, it was actually progress. By eliminating the dependency on another department and eradicating the inefficiencies and

distractions of the inadequate system they were in control of their destiny. Interestingly, they were more efficient with manual processes than the automated ones.

The staff was excited about finally being able to manage their work, problems got resolved and they began delivering the service their customers deserved. Manual processes can be implemented quickly so the operation completely turned around in a month, and they met their service goals for many months afterward. By reducing dependencies they found their stride and moved out of the victim mode. Refusing to lose, THEY WERE WINNERS.

NUISANCE PROBLEMS: It is not unusual to observe leaders talking frequently about nuisance problems, those that churn for years, always there, festering and distracting but not significant enough to generate serious action to resolve them. These nuisances can suck the life out of an operation. People feel weighted down by them. The good news is they are a rich target for employee development.

Publish a list of the problems and ask your team for volunteers to take them on as projects. They provide remarkable opportunities for staff to get experience at leading projects and functioning as effective teams. Since these are nuisance problems and probably not a high priority, monitor closely and require cost benefit analysis on any proposed solutions. Even if resolution is not viable, the team's analysis and evaluation experience alone will make the process worthwhile. Many nuisance problems will be eliminated or at least mitigated somewhat, and staff will gain experience and be winners as opposed to being victims to a bunch of annoying problems.

CALL TO ACTION: Leaders occasionally make an appeal to all employees for something, but do not make a specific *call to action*. Employees get the message but don't know exactly what they are to do about it. If you ask them to increase production, you have got to tell them exactly, in detail, what each one of them must do to achieve that--a specific, measurable action.

Make a point to include a clear message of the *call to action* in your communications, always reinforcing it at the end of the appeal. **People cannot win if they don't know what they must contribute individually to do so.**

TAKE THE POWER: Some leaders wait around for someone to give them the authority to act on a problem or to pursue a new initiative. If a solution is not on the list of priority tactics in their plan for the year or is not officially assigned to them, they dismiss it, missing out on an exceptional opportunity to STAND OUT.

> A new vice president asked his boss what kind of training he would get on being a vice president and how to get a copy of the manual. He was quite shocked to learn that neither existed. Few people realize that the higher up in an organization you go, the less likely there is to be training or documentation on how to do your job. His boss told him this: "**Take the Power.** You see a problem, you fix it. You need to know something, you learn it. You need my help, ask. Come see me every Friday to let me know how your week went, and we will map out a strategy for the next one. In the meantime, I am here if you need me. You are trained."

Victims vs Winners

Once the new vice president got over the shock of this revelation, he took the power and did whatever he thought needed to be done for his department to succeed. The latitude he had in doing this because there were no defined requirements proved to be a tremendous opportunity. Additionally, he made notes as he learned his job and took the initiative to produce documentation for subsequent employees who stepped into the vice presidential role.

If you have a fire in your belly and you pick the winning path, you will play the cards you are dealt. **The less structure and orientation, the more license you have to act in that void and create your own. Take the power.**

As a leader you create the plan, you don't just follow it. You see something that needs to be done, do it. Don't underestimate your power. If no one officially assigns a problem or opportunity to you, take it. **Most bosses would rather jerk your chain occasionally because you overstepped your bounds than to have to push and prod you to take things on.** Just make certain to report to your boss regularly, so he knows what you are doing. He should hear it from you, not someone else. It is important that he is "in the know."

An extraordinary leader is resourceful and enterprising. He will seize the moment. When facing a challenge he thinks, "Bring it on." He goes for the win, and one way or another, he will win. Employees want to win. You owe it to them to ensure that happens. Never lead them down the victim path. Challenge them to find a way to WIN-- NO MATTER WHAT.

LEADERSHIP MISTAKE - 7

Not Recognizing a Leader's ROLE AS NURTURER

Nurture everybody.

Perhaps in the intense, structured world of the business community where power is generally revered, it is difficult to imagine that nurturing people is a top priority for being a strong leader, but it absolutely is. You must nurture your employees, your boss, your peers, your business associates and your customers. It is your job as a leader to nurture everyone around you. A savvy leader is an extraordinary nurturer.

NURTURING EMPLOYEES: Nurturing employees runs the gamut from being sensitive and facilitative, coaching and counseling, showing interest, supporting them through a health or family crisis to sometimes literally saving them from physical harm. It can involve hooking them up with an employee assistance program, referring them to a charitable organization, or visiting them in the hospital. Most of the time, though, nurturing involves small daily sacrifices on your part that make a big difference to employees.

Nurturing

> A college professor who had experience teaching in secondary schools suggested to her college students, who were future teachers, that on bad weather days they resist the temptation to wear dark, gloomy clothes and put on something bright and cheerful. "You won't feel like it," she said, "but you need to do it for your students." How much positive influence does a leader wearing colorful clothes have on employees on a bad weather day? Who knows, but doing so is a small sacrifice.

Little things mean on lot. On snowy days, you can take your leadership team to the employee parking lot and scoop snow and scrape car windows as employees are leaving. When promoting someone or putting them in for a raise, you can walk the paperwork through the system so they go home Friday night and celebrate with their family rather than waiting all weekend to get the news on Monday. These things require little effort, but they mean a lot to others. They are opportunities to show you care about your staff.

Nurturing includes paying attention to how change affects people. Seek ways to help them "lean into change."

> An accuracy measurement was introduced in an area where none existed before. No doubt, there were going to be high error rates, even among seasoned employees. To reduce employee trauma over the change, a *grace period* was established where the only ones who saw a person's accuracy results were the employee and the person measuring it. Employees had a chance to work up to an acceptable level by the time the first official report came out, saving a lot of embarrassment and providing a strong incentive to improve quickly.

Coaching, championing and mentoring are obvious nurturing processes, although they can be problematic when not universally applied and discreetly handled.

MENTORING

Visibly mentoring someone can be perceived as favoritism. This is damaging to the employee you are mentoring as well as to yourself. Without an official mentoring program in your organization, you should probably turn down requests for this level of personal support.

When you mentor, coach, or champion an employee, they almost always tell others, which makes discretion ineffective. To neutralize the favoritism perception, apply employee development support broadly across a range of employees and formalize it. Be inclusive.

NURTURING YOUR BOSS: People are usually surprised by the suggestion of nurturing their boss. It is particularly a good idea if you don't have a good boss, which may be an even more surprising suggestion, but the weaker and less competent your boss, the more important it is that you play the role of nurturer. It is your job to support him in being successful and, more importantly, to ensure the best outcomes possible under the circumstances. This is a loyalty issue, not just to your boss, but to your company, other employees and your customers.

This can be a challenge, but it is simply playing the cards you are dealt. Think of it this way. **You don't just work for your boss, you work for your company. Also, you were there when he came, and you will most likely be there when he is gone.**

Nurturing

It is not your job to "take out" your boss if he is not effective. This does not mean you participate in covering for him if he is doing something wrong, but it does mean you owe him a certain level of loyalty and support as part of your job. Otherwise, you become incompetent right along with him, and you will not look good to others if you bad mouth your boss. You don't necessarily have to defend him, but you should take the high road when talking about him to others.

There is an upside to the misfortune of having a less than competent boss. It is an opportunity to demonstrate you can work for a variety of bosses, you are flexible and stable, and you can endure and persevere. Many people would wipe out. You ride the wave.

If you have a good boss, nurture him as well by seeking his advice and acknowledging his expertise. Nurturing is not politicking. It is supporting and sustaining.

> Nothing makes a boss feel better than to have one of his staff ask his opinion. If you are an action-oriented "go getter," as most leaders are, you tend to do your job independently and rarely seek advice from others. Make a point to bounce things off of your boss. Do the same with peers and other associates if for no other reason than it nurtures them--makes them feel good. When you do, it is likely you will learn more than you expected.

BE A GOOD FOLLOWER: Nurturing your boss requires that you be a good follower. Allow him to manage you, keep him in the loop on what you are doing, determine his requirements, and meet them. Give him a weekly status report, even if he doesn't ask for it. This shows respect. It is also a chance to sell yourself. Invite his input, and do not be resentful when he intervenes. You may think you know more than he does, but odds are you don't, and you will appear arrogant if you project that perception. **A certain amount of deference is required to be a good follower. Following is part of leading. Following is nurturing. To be a good leader, you must also be a good follower.**

NURTURING YOUR PEERS: Be the guy who everyone goes to when they have a bad day. Take them to lunch or out for a bite after work. Be that person.

NURTURING YOUR CUSTOMERS: This goes without saying. I mean, how important is taking care of customers? When making decisions, selecting the option that provides the most value to the customer is almost always the optimal choice. It makes the company stronger.

PEOPLE PRIORITY: When setting your priorities, put the people things at the top of your list. You get something off of your desk that affects only you and one or two other people and no one notices much. When you perform a task that removes a barrier and facilitates your staff, you set off serious exponential progress, and the impact is profound.

Get merit increases in on time, install that recognition program, get those interviews done, fill that vacancy, promote someone, put a newsletter out, and participate in training. Make certain everyone on your management team has a project over and above their normal duties. Be all over any problem that inhibits employees' ability to get their jobs done. If you do not, you can incur extensive waste as people wait around for their leader to do something. The bottom line is, you can facilitate progress, or get in the way of it.

PEOPLE FIRST

If you can't get everything done you need to do in a day, do the people things during regular working hours and the paper work and solitary activities off hours. Arrive at work a few hours before employees so you can organize your day, work your desk, and stand ready to be available.

Don't close your door, screen visitors or shut people out. Return communications promptly. Always be accessible. Your objective is to keep everyone else going. Interact, assign tasks, set up work groups, walk the floors, attend meetings, facilitate problem resolution, and remove barriers to progress.

Often we get caught up in our own career track and our focus is on personal success, but the success of others is just as important. Make your boss successful, and he will champion you and pull you up with him. Make your employees successful and, not only will you experience the joy of watching them shine, you will have their loyalty and support. Nurture customers by taking exceptional care of them and the company does well and everyone wins.

Nurturing is your ace in the hole. Many leaders don't see it as important beyond the political benefits to themselves, but savvy leaders know that honest, sincere nurturing makes you a STAND OUT leader. It sets you apart. It is a key component of the concept of leadership as *service* **to others.**

LEADERSHIP MISTAKE - 8

Too Much Focus on THE JOB YOU WANT

*You must do the job you've got
before you can get the one you want.*

It is natural if you are ambitious to always have your eye out for the next opportunity, but in doing so you run the risk of becoming distracted from the job you have. Still, it is appropriate, even recommended, that you target your next career move. Just remember the prospect of achieving that desired result depends on doing the job you've got well.

> An information technology graduate took a job pulling staples in a mailroom because the job market was so bad. His employer knew he was over-qualified and was open to him taking the position with the intent of eventually moving into the technical area. In the meantime, though, the boss suggested he be the best staple puller they ever had. At that company you could not get the job you wanted if you didn't do the one you've got well.

Historically, politicking to get ahead worked, but there is more emphasis today on whether a person delivers the goods. More importantly, do you really want to be the guy who got ahead because of who he knew? Would you not rather be the one who got ahead because he deserved it?

Employees who are so focused on promotions that they don't do the job they've got are ill-informed or simply not willing to do the work to get ahead. You promote one of these people and you demoralize a lot of others.

The best way to schmooze, is to participate in corporate activities, volunteer for projects, dress and act more professional than the masses, nurture and champion others, and do your job well.

> When you get off of the elevator, you want the president or any other executive present to ask the remaining employees who you are because you look sharp and serious, and he wonders what you do. The information you want him to get next is that you are a respected, strong performer at whatever it is you are doing. He already knows from the way you look that you mean business. Your reputation does the rest.

Don't be the guy who politics his way to the top. Don't buy into the "it's who you know, not what you do" concept. You may occasionally realize some success from that approach, but you will not have the respect of others. Just as important, doing the job you've got is a matter of self-respect. When you do get that promotion, you want to see the word "deserving" in all the congratulatory emails.

LEADERSHIP MISTAKE - 9

Failure to Articulate the PURPOSE OF WORK

*People need to know that what they **personally** do every day is meaningful work.*

It should be no surprise that employees need to have a *sense of purpose* about work. Where most leaders miss the boat is that they only talk about the purpose of the company. They sell the company vision, goals, and direction. That is important, but what an employee really needs to understand is how the tasks he performs fit into all that. What is the purpose of what **he does**?

GOAL TRANSLATION

Anytime a goal is set by the company, translate it down to the departmental level and then to the employee level. Be specific about interpreting what actions each employee contributes to meeting that goal through their daily work processes. Involve them in determining what that is.

A vital contributor to an employee buying into goals is his ability to attach meaning to them. Before you can help employees internalize a *sense of purpose* around what they do, you must have one yourself, something that inspires passion. This is more specific and personal than the company line. It is how you feel about your work, your leadership role, and what you and your team deliver. Articulate your personal *sense of purpose* to others.

DEPARTMENT TRANSLATION: Use the company vision and mission to establish a framework specific to your department. In concert with your staff, chart your course by defining the following, which establishes a context within which all employees in your area operate:

PURPOSE -- Why the department exists and why employees are doing what they are doing.

VISION -- Where your department is headed.

MISSION -- What the department does to get there.

PLANS, STRATEGIES AND TACTICS -- Specific actions directed at accomplishing the mission.

VALUES -- Who you are and how you act while you are doing it.

Center what you do at work every day around this framework, review it often, and translate it down to the individual and what he does.

Here is an extra bonus from this activity: It is a tremendously effective communication tool. **You can use this information to demonstrate to your boss your vision for the operation, and he and you will have the language to articulate it to others. You will hear him telling the president what you are about, and the marketing staff** will speak of your vision and mission to customers. It is also a vehicle to obtain support from others upon whom you are dependent. This is powerful stuff.

EMPLOYEE TRANSLATION: Communicate both the company and department purpose, vision, mission, plans, strategies, tactics and core values to all employees. Any goals require translation down to the individual employee's work processes detailing specifically what he is to do. For example:

> "Every work unit is to be executed perfectly. Verify all information. Review the check list before you finish the transaction, so you don't leave out any steps. If you are not sure of something, ask. Don't guess. To meet the goal each employee must on the average produce at least 30 units per hour with 99% accuracy. By exceeding the goal, you can participate in the employee incentive plan. The top ten performers will be recognized in the monthly honors program."

INSPIRING A SENSE OF PURPOSE: For a sense of purpose to resonate, employees need an emotional link, something that relates to people. Don't make something up. If you analyze work functions thoroughly, you can find the people factor in every function performed. It makes a difference to someone, otherwise there would be no reason to be doing it.

Seek a meaningful example of how employees' work affects other people and use it to convey a *sense of purpose* every chance you get. Paint a picture. Here is an example of a customer service picture that relates work to people:

Purpose of Work

> "The mother of a small boy who has cancer and is on a treatment plan of chemotherapy should not have to put on her list of things to do to call us because we didn't do something right or on time. If her little guy is having a bad day, she needs to be taking care of him. If he is having a good day, she needs to enjoy him. She does not know how much longer she will have him. There are situations like this in the work on your desk, families in severe emotional and financial crisis. You will touch them with how you do your job every minute of every day. This is purposeful work. There are people behind the computer screens who are counting on us. Take care of them."

You can even go so far as to tell problem employees, "If you don't care about these people, you can't work here." When an employee does not care about customers and cannot embrace a *sense of purpose* in relation to them, they are clearly not demonstrating the core values of your organization.

MISSION STATEMENTS: Companies often have a mission statement, a description of what they are about. Departments should also have a crisp mission statement specific to the functions performed in that area. These can serve as another avenue for instilling purpose. **Everyone should know the significance of their role in accomplishing the mission.** It is vital that department leaders engage the support of everyone in the company in carrying out their mission.

> The management team of a service unit was successful at getting the organization to agree that customer service staff had direct access to anyone in the company to resolve a service issue. They also had permission to seek out other sources outside the company. Every employee knew what he had to do

Purpose of Work

each day to deliver on the mission statement, and his leaders engaged everyone else in the company to support accomplishing it.

Anyone should be able to ask any employee about his department's mission, and the employee can state it and describe his role in achieving it. **There is often confusion around the distinguishing definitions of mission, goals, and objectives as the differences are somewhat subtle. Don't let that bog you down. Just come up with something that works for the employees and use it.**

> Mail room employees in a company defined their mission as: **"Never lose mail--ever."** Then, they set a goal: **"To deliver all mail within twenty four hours--no exceptions."** You could walk up to any employee in the area and ask them about their mission and goal and they would state them. They could also tell you their specific role in the process of accomplishing them.
>
> In addition, they had a clear *sense of purpose*. They knew others in the company were counting on them and that there was tremendous waste if they did not deliver. They also understood the impact they had on the customer.
>
> Processes were set up to ensure they accomplished their mission and goal. They began flowing manpower with the work, sending employees to the sorting area when the mail flooded in and then into the scanning area. Next they shifted resources into delivery mode. Everyone knew every function so if an employee was out, someone else could do the work and do it well.
>
> Everyone's desk was set up to ensure a consistent process. Anyone could work any desk. Mail flowed through specific places in the department and only in those places so nothing was lost. Strategies were

developed for holiday mail fluctuations, bad weather days, and unexpected employee absences. Management sought exceptions to corporate policies so work hours could be shifted to match mail delivery and flow.

In the hiring process, it was difficult to evaluate whether an applicant had the dexterity and speed to handle mail efficiently, so temps were used to fill vacancies. Only the strongest performers were hired. The temp costs were more than offset by elimination of costs and risks associated with mis-hires.

The company was so proud of this operation that when board members or executives from other firms visited, they were given a tour of the mailroom. Can you imagine an executive saying to another executive, "You have got to see our mail room!" It was a model for the rest of the company. Who would have thought the mailroom would achieve that kind of status? A *sense of purpose* at both the management and employee level was the key to this accomplishment

Set the context for the work being done in each of your departments. Articulate mission statements and clear objectives. Identify the purpose of work. Find the meaning in it. Convey how it affects people who are counting on that work being done well, and constantly remind employees of the importance of that. A *sense of purpose* **is a powerful force and a gift to employees. It creates an awareness of the opportunity to** *serve*--**to make a difference for others by doing a job well.**

LEADERSHIP MISTAKE - 10

Undervaluing the PEOPLE COMPONENT

Everything you or your organization does affects people. Everything.

There is a people component to everything that happens in your organization--every change, communication, action or in-action. As a leader, assessing the people ramifications of everything you deal with all day every day and determining if any action is required in relation to employees will set your organization apart. Activities run more smoothly, enhanced outcomes materialize, and *employee loyalty* flourishes.

PEOPLE PLANNING: Regardless of how well you execute change, if you don't have a plan for the people component, you are going to have problems. Time invested in including people impact analysis and *people planning* in change processes is offset by minimizing trauma to employees. Don't wait for them to react to things. Proactively anticipate potential reactions and develop strategies to address them. **Include managing the people component as a step in every project action plan. In fact,**

The People Component

consider any change as a project worthy of people planning, coordination, and communication.

In the face of massive change, it will not be the mechanics of the change process that create the biggest challenge. It will be the people component. Employees are intensely distracted not only with the change itself, but with the simple anticipation of it. As a result, productivity takes a dive, turnover climbs steeply, and morale sinks. This can be paralyzing. By including *people impact analysis* and *people planning* in change processes, these ramifications can be significantly mitigated.

Without solid leadership, employees react and over-react to even the smallest incidents. No change is required, just the suggestion of it. It is astonishing how insecure employees can be, and insecurity is a huge distraction. It dampens the spirit. The most valued employee, who would be the last person to go, is certain he is going to lose his job any day now. Employees may know they are valuable, but do they know that you know it?

> A woman worked for a company where praise and recognition were rare. She knew she did a good job, but was certain no one noticed. She was discouraged but persevered, focusing on taking care of her staff and customers and delivering solid outcomes. One day the president came into her office, a rare occasion, and said, "I want you to know you are a valuable *key player* in this organization." What he said rocked her world. It meant a lot.
>
> It occurred to her that she had employees working for her who possibly did not realize that she considered them *key players*, so she set out to tell

them. She asked the leaders in her division to do the same and to do it every time they noticed someone playing a key role. Recognizing and acknowledging valuable employees as *key players* demonstrates you are tuned in to the people component.

People are a priority. Let them know how much you value them and be constantly contemplating what they need. **Make *people planning* part of your processes all day every day. In addition to having it as an action step in project plans, always have activities that support people on your "To Do" list. Be on a constant quest for opportunities to personally thank and appreciate employees.**

COMMUNICATION: This is huge. An integral part of providing people support for project processes and the resulting changes is frequent, intense, and comprehensive communication to and from employees. All the other planning in the world will count for nothing if you don't have a communication strategy. Not doing communication well is incapacitating. Here are some things you can do:

- **Set the context.** Frame every project for employees. Inform them of the purpose and objectives as well as what the project and its outcomes mean to them. Document and review this context information periodically. People are easily distracted by details of a project and forget the overview. Don't sugar coat negative aspects of the endeavor. Instead, inspire staff to seek solutions and meet any challenges as the winners they are. The important thing is to not surprise them. Anticipate and neutralize to the extent you can any negative consequences generated by change.

- **Define project mechanics.** Work with project leaders to document the mechanics for running projects and communicate them at project kick-off meetings. Sell project processes to the teams and everyone affected by them. This includes such things as: approach, team structure, roles and responsibilities, how the team will function, the product to be delivered, time lines, reporting requirements, and communication processes. Emphasize the need to include *people planning* in every project.

- **Solicit feedback.** Constantly seek feedback from project team members as well as those affected by any changes. You and project leaders should end each communication or meeting with a request for questions and concerns and respond to them with vigor. Team members and other employees will identify issues and steps critical to the project. **Don't be afraid of Q&A. You don't have to know all the answers, but you sure want to know what all the questions are**. Savvy leaders are on a constant quest for feedback.

- **Formalize communications:** If you do not schedule communication opportunities up front, they will not happen. Schedule routine staff and team meetings. Generate minutes with assignments for meetings so everyone clearly knows what action steps are their responsibility. Require that they report on them at the next meeting. This ensures that things get done. Set a fixed date to produce a newsletter each month. Commit to all-employee town hall meetings at pre-scheduled times and places. Schedule recognition events. Pay careful attention to targeting appropriate receivers of each communication and err on the side of inclusion.

- **Publish a calendar.** Include all project activities, communications, and events in on a calendar and identify a point person for each.

- **Stand up meetings:** It is important to have avenues to disseminate information expediently. It is not practical to have a formal meeting for every communication, yet people need to hear information timely and directly from an authoritative source. A *stand up meeting* is a valuable tool in these instances. Keep a list of things you want to share and gather employees around in the work areas or halls and have short meetings. This discourages rumors, and with Q&A it encourages timely feedback. Employees love stand up meetings. They appreciate the fact that you care enough to come to them and personally convey information.

- **Employees as credible messengers:** People of influence in the work areas who are not formal leaders can be credible, expedient communication channels. Establish a process to convey information through *peer leaders*. They know what employees need to hear. Use them as advisors when developing messages, and seek their feedback on how messages are being received.

- **Elevator speeches:** As you are commuting to work each day, consider topical questions employees have on their minds. Develop messages so short they can be delivered between floors on an elevator or in hallway conversations. Have your leadership team do the same. People receiving information in an informal setting will feel they have inside information directly from an important source, and it will be broadly shared.

PEOPLE THINGS FIRST: Don't let people issues linger or fester. You can't do people interaction on off hours. Be available to employees during the day. Walk the floors and attend meetings. When people enter your office greet them with a cheery smile no matter how distracted you are or how bad your day is going.

APPRECIATION: Stand ready to react to every accomplishment. Don't say "I appreciate **it**." Say "I appreciate **you**." Then, go the extra mile and tell the employee's boss how capable they are, especially if they are in another division. Very few people do this, and when you do, you will STAND OUT. Soon you will observe others modeling your behavior.

HOOPLA: Put on playful, big deal recognition events with music, skits, and outrageous fun around honoring and recognizing employees. It may be a sacrifice and a lot of work to do it, but employees love hoopla. Few opportunities allow you to visibly demonstrate your dedication to the troops better than a big blast event. Participate fully, enthusiastically, and visibly.

You won't find a more striking example of synergy than a good leader facilitating the troops and turning them loose. Never undervalue the *people component* of what is happening in your organization. Savvy leaders anticipate the people impact of every change and proactively plan accordingly. Investing in *people planning* is investing in people. It smooths the way for them and softens the blows of change. It is *serving* those you lead.

10 MANAGEMENT MYTHS

MANAGEMENT MYTH - 1

Anything Worth Doing Is Worth Doing Well

The Reality: *Sometimes perfection is not worth the price. Imperfect solutions might be better than waiting for the ultimate perfect one.*

An old expression says, "Anything worth doing is worth doing well," the well implying perfection. The reality is sometimes you have to do something, anything, to make the situation better, even if it is not the ultimate solution. **Seeking perfection can be paralyzing.** This is especially true when you are dependent on others over whom you have limited control and who are not focused on perfection. This means settling for a fix that is not perfect. You cannot NOT do the interim fix because it is not the ultimate fix. If you do not settle, a number of people are going to be seriously hassled for a long time, and one of them is going to be you.

Even quality programs where the goal is to do everything right every time temper that premise with suggestions of temporary fixes that are not perfect solutions. You must face the reality that there are instances where the ultimate outcome may not be achievable. If this disturbs you too much, you may lead your team down the victim path. **Get what you can get.** Pursue the best solution later, while realizing it may not be perfect either. It is an imperfect world. Seeking perfection can result in unfortunate decisions and significant opportunity costs.

> Occasionally a perfectionist student drops a class because they can't pull an A intending to repeat the class later in hopes of getting a better result. This decision adds a semester to their stint in college. They give up four months of experience and income at a high dollar job once they graduate to get an A instead of a B, and there is no guarantee they will get an A the next time around.
>
> Most potential employers don't care if a grade is an A or B. Still, the student maintains that anything worth doing is worth doing well. Perhaps he should consider that a B is "well." At any rate, it is a costly, impractical decision to drop the class and start over. Making such decisions in the business world might cause someone to question your judgement.

Perfection is always the ultimate goal. Reality is the ultimate challenge. Never give up on a perfect solution, but recognize that incremental fixes and imperfect solutions may be better than waiting for the perfect ones.

The opportunity costs of perfection are sometimes not worth it. Make your decisions through the application of rational thought, practical evaluation, and prudent judgement. Savvy leaders understand the price of perfection and the value of alternative options.

MANAGEMENT MYTH - 2

Always Be Fair

The Reality: *You Can't Get to Fair. Fairness Is In the Eye of the Beholder.*

You can't get to fair for everybody because everyone interprets fairness differently. What is perceived as fair by one person might be construed as unfair by another.

You cannot always treat every employee the same because situations are rarely the same. Even if they were the same and you treated them just alike, someone would see that as unfair believing their own situation is different or special. Fairness is always your ultimate goal, but the reality is that it is virtually impossible to accommodate everyone's interpretation of it.

> When you have to decide between two employees for a promotion where one is the strongest performer and the other has been there the longest, do what is best for the customer, the company, the common good of all employees, and the department. Select the strongest performer.

The employee with seniority and those who support him will most likely conclude this is unfair. However, if you select the person with the most seniority, the higher performer will conclude that is unfair. Additionally, you send a message to the troops that to get ahead, all you have to do is be there, and it doesn't matter how you perform. It goes without saying, you don't want to send that message.

Work with the senior employee who didn't get the job to improve his performance so he becomes competitive. Put the ball in his court to do what is required to get promoted and support him in that endeavor. You might be surprised what he can do once he knows clearly what is required to get ahead.

FAIRNESS AWARENESS: Proactively communicate to employees how the process of selection works and remind them they do not have all the information that goes into decisions. It would be unfair to applicants for you to share that information with everyone. Ask for their trust that you are selecting people resources that produce the best outcomes for the customer, the company, the common good of all employees, and the department.

A good leader makes every effort to be even handed, but employees will realize that only if he creates awareness. They may not have thought of the common good and have no concept that doing what is best for the customer is most often best for everyone. Individual sacrifice for the good of all and earning a promotion through producing results might not be on their radar either. That is not all.

Fairness

The relationship of high productivity and efficient operations to competitive pricing in the market place is also unlikely to be on their minds, but it should be. Those end results drive the company's success. It is up to you as their leader to educate them on these big picture realities.

How you handle employees who did not get a job is critically important. It needs to be a generous coaching conversation. Advise them that how they respond to not being chosen may determine whether they are a serious candidate the next time around. Because management staff must maintain a positive attitude in the face of constant disappointment, aspiring applicants must demonstrate they can rise above unfortunate circumstances and remain focused and committed.

Encourage employees to maintain a positive attitude and do the things they need to do to earn a promotion and to compete effectively for it. Support them in that endeavor while always being candid about their prospects and steering them toward viable possibilities. Under no circumstances should you suggest a career path that is not realistic.

Sometimes you have to inspire people to be the best they can be at whatever it is they are already doing. Look for ways to enhance their work assignments and to tap into whatever talents they possess. If they have applied for a promotion, they clearly have the desire to do more meaningful work. Give it to them.

It is important you are clear in your own mind about how fairness works so you can explain it to employees. They have most likely bought into the myth that you must always be fair and have no concept of the improbability of that happening. Also, they will most likely have a very narrow personal perspective around this issue that does not include the concept of fairness to customers or other employees.

Don't be distracted from good business decisions by fairness issues. This is not kindergarten, and you are not entertaining arguments over who has the most Kool-Aid in their cup. You have purposeful work to do. In the process of doing that, you will be as fair as you can be to everyone while putting fairness to customers and the common good first.

MANAGEMENT MYTH - 3

Protect Your Staff from Adversity

The Reality: *Adversity can be a valuable mechanism for engaging employees.*

Adversity can be a tool to inspire teams to pull together. Although a leader can provide a buffer between employees and unfortunate events, sometimes that is appropriate and sometimes it is not. An external challenge to your operation can be an opportunity to show what your team can do when the chips are down, to demonstrate they can win no matter what. Don't underestimate their willingness to rise to the occasion.

No one looks forward to threats and challenges, but they can provide an opportunity to create a cohesive, energized work force. Refuse to succumb to the hopelessness and the negative. Don't go down the victim path. Go down the warrior one. **You see a challenge headed your direction, you think, "bring it on" and engage your staff in doing the same.**

When marketing informs you of a competitor threat, fire up the troops. Decide that anything your competition can do, you can do even better.

When someone displays a lack of confidence in what your staff can do, inspire them to prove the person wrong. They are a lean, mean running machine and they know it. They win--no matter what. Don't protect your staff from adversity and rob them of the opportunity to win.

Make sure any threat you tap into is real and relevant, and never create situations with the intention of motivating staff. There will be enough real adversity to deal with. You don't have to invent any.

COPING WITH ADVERSITY: If you are a leader you will occasionally have people in your office crying their eyes out thinking it is the end of the world because something is not going well. Reminded them that, "It is **just work**. No one was injured and no one died." Get them to look at the situation rationally rather than emotionally.

WORST-CASE SCENARIO

When adversity strikes and someone is severely stressed, an effective coping mechanism is to have the person contemplate the worst-case scenario that can materialize under the circumstance. Next, figure out what he can do in that situation and what that looks like. He will most likely realize it is not the catastrophe he imagined in the first place, and once there is a plan for the worst outcome, he can focus on more likely ones.

Depending on the circumstances, many times employees will be comforted to understand the magnitude of your support. They may have been sold out by superiors in the past. You can say, "If the worst-case scenario materializes on this project, I may get chewed out, but it will not be the first time and probably won't be the last. I can take it." Don't fail to hold employees accountable for outcomes, but anytime you take the emotion and fear out of their reaction, you can get them back on track.

EMOTIONAL AWARENESS: When facing adversity or failure, some employees become emotional. Times have changed, and it is no longer the kiss of death to cry at work. When someone does so, hand them a tissue. Do not write off anyone's career because they showed emotion. However, if crying is a common response, consider a plan to raise their emotional awareness.

EMOTIONAL INTELLIGENCE

Self-awareness and the ability to interpret, regulate, and manage the emotions of oneself, others, and groups are tied to a person's level of emotional intelligence (EI). Although there is some controversy over the concept of EI and its application in the business environment, an understanding of it is helpful in managing employees. There is considerable support for the proposition that people can increase their EI through awareness, which in turn contributes to their ability to manage feelings, guide actions in a more productive manner, and deal with adversity.

Adversity

When a threat surfaces, it is natural to want to be gentle with your staff, but you are not seeking a parent/child relationship. Employees will act like children when you treat them like children. They are stronger than they seem. Be real, candid, and forthright. **Don't underestimate employees' ability to deal with adversarial situations and bad information. Just don't leave a leadership void once they are faced with these challenges.**

On the occasions when your team realizes a bad outcome, focus everyone on *the rally*. A look back for root cause analysis is always appropriate, but aside from that, set their sights on looking forward to preventative strategies, progress, and future opportunities for success--the next win. Remind them that no matter what the outcome, the situation was better because they engaged and gave it their all. The team held together and supported each other.

Adverse situations are where DO SOMETHING MANAGEMENT really kicks in. Take the power. Own it. Fix it. Be all over it. Savvy leaders face adversity head on and develop a strategy to move forward. Part of that strategy involves getting the troops on board. You cannot do that if you protect them from the reality of the adversity. People are often at their best in times of challenge. Don't deprive them of that opportunity.

MANAGEMENT MYTH - 4

Always Defend Your Employees

The Reality: *Don't defend indefensible behavior.*

The old premise that you always stand up for your employees and defend them no matter what is an unfortunate platitude. You should not defend indefensible behavior, and employees should not expect you to do so as a matter of integrity--yours and theirs. They must be accountable and face their mistakes or inappropriate behavior and any related consequences head on. **Employees also need to know that although you are not going to defend them, you will support them in salvaging the situation and redeeming themselves.**

BAD BEHAVIOR: Inappropriate behavior should never be defended. If you defend bad behavior, you encourage more of it. You will have a department full of people who act inappropriately and treat others badly. **Keep in mind that tolerating bad behavior is endorsing it.**

A manager in a leadership training class asked the instructor what he should do when his employees lie to him. The instructor was stunned by the question and replied, "An employee would lie to me only twice, and the second time I would fire him. That's what you should do, and you need to tell your employees that and follow through." This manager was tolerating negative employee behavior and therefore endorsing it, sending the message it is okay to lie.

Employees lie when it works. Lying is a blatant display of disrespect. Whether it works or not depends on the leader. Lying is also a form of manipulation, especially lying by omission. A leader's inaction gives the liar a positive payoff and endorses the behavior. Lying is a serious integrity issue. **If you cannot count on the word of your associates, you cannot lead effectively.**

BAD OUTCOMES: If you find yourself repeatedly dealing with bad outcomes, it is time to figure out ways to get good ones rather than investing in defending people and explaining what happened.

EXTERNALIZATION

Some employees look for ways to blame bad outcomes on others. They are extremely creative at coming up with excuses other than their own accountability, and it is easy to find someone else to blame.

They will also "throw up decoys" to distract from their involvement, meaning when confronted they will try to change the focus to another person, incident or issue. They

Defending Employees

may even throw the focus back on you, perhaps in an attack mode, just to distract from themselves. Don't accept this behavior. Call them on it and insist they accept responsibility. Whether the employee works for you or someone else, make certain they know you see the decoy for what it is, and you are not buying it.

When something bad happens, it is not unusual for management to become preoccupied with a vigorous defense at the expense of pursuing a solution. Savvy leaders don't invest in defending bad outcomes when the root cause was the result of action or inaction by themselves or their staff. **It is not about the defense. It is about the fix.**

Naive employees will occasionally cover up mistakes rather than report them, an action reflecting poor judgement. This precludes any prospect of correcting the problem, and the mistake will most likely be discovered at some point. New employees and young people are bad about this. Save them the anguish by including requirements for reporting in employee training. Explain that the consequences for hiding a mistake are more severe than those for the mistake itself.

You cannot build strong teams in an environment where bad behavior and bad outcomes are ignored and thereby defended and endorsed. Make certain employees understand you will defend them when they are right, and when they are not, you will provide support to salvage the situation and work to redeem them. Convince them to face problems head on with full disclosure and accountability so they can be *stand up* employees.

MANAGEMENT MYTH - 5

Conflict is Inevitable

The Reality: *The path to conflict avoidance is awareness and employee development.*

Conflict happens, but it is not inevitable. When employees have a clear awareness of core values and the behaviors that support them, disagreements don't involve conflict. Consensus is achievable when employees know how to TEAM UP. If they do not, conflict prevails and it is paralyzing. **The frequency and intensity of conflict among employees is directly correlated to the effectiveness of the organization's leadership.**

> The leader of a department maintained that consensus is rarely possible. You can be sure that was a true statement under that circumstance. He withheld information, showed little interest in anyone else's perspective, and was not inclined to compromise. He was dismissive of others, avoided team participation, and did not dissent peacefully. Needless to say, his working relationships with other departments were not positive. There was

constant conflict with his area and many victims of his attitude, including his own staff.

Human nature as it is, conflict in groups is so common that it is unusual if there is none. As a leader, you can counteract this tendency. The path to conflict avoidance and consensus building is awareness and employee development. Here is what you can do to prevent conflict in your organization:

-Introduce core values and a behavioral model.

-Orient staff on personality behavioral patterns and emotional intelligence.

-Train on teamwork, consensus building and conflict avoidance.

These training applications are powerful employee development opportunities that provide dividends in a host of areas. They are well worth the investment. In addition to teaching employees how to TEAM UP and reach consensus, this knowledge enhances personal relationships. Awareness paves the way to cooperation and collaboration.

THE ROAD TO CONSENSUS

An optimal business decision everyone can support almost always reveals itself when:

(1) all relevant information is shared, and

(2) all perspectives are presented, valued and acknowledged.

The prospect of consensus is extremely high under these circumstances. On the other hand, it is highly unlikely when information is not shared and/or every stakeholder's perspective is not represented.

When considering all perspectives, a hierarchy can guide decision making and consensus building. **In most situations it is best to consider the customer perspective first, the company second, the company's employee base third, and the department last.**

This implies that department sacrifices have to be made for the good of the whole and recognizes that if the whole is not doing well, no one else is going to do well either. **When the sacrifice is too great, disclose and discuss, but once a decision is made, you must support it.** Even if you maintain your dissenting opinion, never sabotage a project.

THE SILO EFFECT

When employees refuse to value the perspectives of other departments or the customer and are unwilling to sacrifice for the good of the whole, conflict is rampant, consensus unlikely, and core values are not expressed. Their universe is themselves, their department, and a desire for control. This is known as the silo effect.

Displays of the *silo effect* suggest the employees' leader is modeling the behavior or at least endorsing it by ignoring it. This is tremendously inhibiting to expedient and optimal outcomes.

Conflict

Two departments were embroiled in conflict over which system to procure for a vital task. Both held their positions firmly, each having independently analyzed both systems. A huge conflict evolved and nothing got done. Finally, a team member shared for the first time details on the capabilities of the system he favored. This changed everything. The optimal business decision became obvious and everyone immediately favored his choice. Months of unnecessary conflict had occurred because the group did not team up and everyone didn't have the same information.

Formalizing proposals from teams can ensure that employees seeking approval TEAM UP and have a solid basis for their recommendations, that they have shared all information and considered every relevant perspective.

PROPOSAL FORMAT
Ensure better decisions by requiring proposals be brought forward in a standard format that has categories for alternatives, the pros and cons of each, the perspective of all stakeholders, and documentation of any dissenting opinions. When people have to justify dissenting opinions in a document, they are often more valid and better thought out. Even more important, this process frequently exposes hidden agendas.

Whether you use a form or not, when making important decisions, require from work groups all relevant information, the perspectives of all stakeholders, and disclosure of dissenting opinions.

When conflict is brewing, mentally get out of the moment. Turn yourself into an objective observer of the behavior and focus on redirecting the team toward the task at hand. Most often conflict occurs when someone feels they are not being heard or their competence is being challenged. Unfortunately, it can also be the result of the climate created by leaders.

If you have people in your organization who expect conflict and even seem to thrive on it, who believe consensus is rarely possible and are always ready for a fight, who withhold information and are unwilling to value other areas' perspectives, you will rarely get consensus. Something is fundamentally wrong with this organization.

Even though a leader may operate in that fashion, you can be certain many of his employees are struggling with that. Form alliances with them where possible, but be cautious about visibly championing them when they respond. You may put them in jeopardy with their leader for working with you in a positive manner.

If employee behavior ever rises to the level of bullying, apply a zero tolerance approach. Bullying would fall outside the realm of any core value behavior and has no place in the work environment.

Conflict is debilitating and consensus powerful. As a savvy leader, you create and nurture a positive work environment, keep your core values and behavioral requirements at the forefront, and use your influence to ensure everyone is heard and all relevant information shared. Require that employees TEAM UP. De-personalize any conflict, seek optimal business solutions, and provide orientation on consensus building and teamwork. Pave the way to consensus through enlightenment.

MANAGEMENT MYTH - 6

Employees Don't Like Work Measurement

The Reality: *Some employees like it-- the strongest performers.*

Depending on the volume of work, scale of operations, and type of work, organizations often must employ work measurement systems as a tool to measure quality and production. Measurement programs run the gamut from formal to almost non-existent, but most companies have some basis to evaluate employee performance and the quality of the product or service produced. These measures are typically tied to employee appraisals and salary merits.

Work measurement gets a bad rap. Managers struggle with applying it, and employees often resent it. Here is the big surprise. Who likes it? The strong performers. How else is anyone going to know how good they are? **When you are doing something that makes your strong performers happy and poor performers unhappy, you are on the right track.**

Work Measurement

Work measurement is a complex process. It personally impacts the people involved in it. In a production environment it is an intense measurement of work, unit-by-unit and minute-by-minute. Most programs involve both production and accuracy components, which are mutually exclusive in most people's minds (more about that later). All this makes measurement a challenge to administer, but done well, it offers an incredibly valuable key to delivering a quality product and efficient production.

Measurement allows strong performers to shine; it sets them apart. They will embrace almost any productivity challenge you throw at them and deliver. It is your job as the leader to use measurement to make certain they get the recognition they deserve. It is also your job to deal with those who cannot or will not perform at acceptable levels.

Most of your staff will most likely fall in between these two categories. Don't ignore these people. They provide your best opportunity for improvement. The hotshots are already there. The non-performers are not going to be around in the future unless they improve. Consequently, the people in the middle are your real, shot at performance improvement.

A common challenge when administering work measurement is that anytime steps are taken to improve productivity or accuracy, the expectancies of what employees deliver are increased. This may not go over well, but that depends on how you communicate it.

> An employee once complained, "You are always increasing my production requirements." The answer was "Yes," followed by a long pause indicating that was the answer, period, and in reality it is. **Productivity and accuracy improvement are**

continuous processes. To be competitive in the market place, businesses must constantly evolve and improve, reacting to the unrelenting pressures to produce more with less and controlling costs while at the same time delivering a superior product. This is the nature of business--a matter of survival in a free market. Few employees have any concept of this.

This is where you come in. Create awareness of how the free enterprise model works, and how employees are personally in competition with everyone who is producing in the industry. Convince them they want to win, what is in it for them, and what must be done to do so. Emphasize the value of a strong, competitive company with earnings to support raises, benefits, and job security.

The company does not invests in system enhancements, efficiency initiatives, and quality improvement so employees can slow down and take it easy, but rather so they can produce more units per hour or a better product or service. It is the employees' job to deliver that, and when they do, everyone wins. When they don't, there is significant waste and unfortunate challenges.

THE BUDGET/COST/COMPETITION CONNECTION: You might be surprised how many employees are not aware that you are operating under the constraints of a budget, or at least not why you have one. They believe there is an unlimited supply of money in the organization.

While creating awareness of the free enterprise/competition aspects of business, it is wise to include education on the economics of business, the mandate to manage costs and the implications of that to the company's health and possibly even its survival. If you don't explain that cost containment is a primary factor in your company's product being competitively priced, it is unlikely to occur to employees. Communicate your budget goals and seek their contribution to meeting them through productivity and elimination of waste.

The processes involved in work measurement can naturally be intimidating and many leaders make the mistake of using measurement as a hammer. Savvy leaders do not do this. They use it as enlightenment and motivation, issuing challenges, not threats, and dedicating themselves to coaching, supporting and recognizing those who meet the challenge. **They know for certain who their strong performers are, and they make sure everyone else knows it. In turn, they are firm in their requirement that all employees deliver the quality of work that ensures the company is competitive and sustainable.**

In addition to educating employees, it is important to communicate to prospective employees in the employment interview process the challenges of the environment in which they are going to be working. If you make it clear up front in the interview that employees will be expected to work hard and will be constantly monitored and challenged, but the rewards will be great, slackers will not be interested. Go getters will light up.

For a business to survive, it must be in a constant state of improvement in response to free market competition. Savvy leaders, make certain their employees understand that. They support them in dealing with the ramifications of work management and coping with the constant demands for improvement, while inspiring them to win and rewarding them when they do.

MANAGEMENT MYTH - 7

If You Work Faster, You Will Make More Mistakes

The Reality: *A faster pace will often improve accuracy.*

Because productivity is a key component in the ongoing viability of a company, leaders are always pressing employees to improve it--to work faster. At first blush it seems obvious that if you work faster your error rate will increase, that quality will suffer to some extent. In some situations that is true, but in most it is not. Here is why:

> When a person is geared, trucking, focused, and in a heightened state of concentration, his awareness level is so high that he actually pays more attention to detail than when he is coasting along. Also, he gets a rhythm going that is compatible with applying step-by-step procedures, and he is less likely to leave something out. Under these circumstances, accuracy can actually improve.

Employees will often protest when higher productivity goals are set, maintaining that accuracy will suffer. This is the deal: **If they don't leave out any steps in the process, but do them faster, their accuracy level should not decrease. In fact, there is a high probability it will increase.**

This does seem counter-intuitive, but it is possible to increase productivity with no decline in quality. The challenge is to convince employees of this. You may have to convince some of your managers and supervisors as well. Have them test it out. **The key is to not leave out steps in the process when output is increased.**

Many employees have a work ethic that includes a willingness to apply themselves wholeheartedly to any task. A savvy leader looks for that work ethic when hiring, but there are always employees who view anything related to applying themselves diligently to work as a negative.

> Some employees work harder at getting out of work than if they did the work in the first place. Time passes slowly and they cannot feel good about their day. Most people who do this have simply not viewed their work in any other way.
>
> If you can convince them to try for a week to knock the work out, to get that concentration, to feel the rhythm of production and then make note of how the hours go by quicker and how they feel about what they did when they go home at night, you will very likely see a whole new person at the end of the experiment. Praise them for their evolution. Who knows how far they can go. They may turn out to be your strongest performers.

People are highly driven by expectancies. A savvy leader knows that you will not realize high standards of performance if you don't expect them. The leader's vision of what employees can do determines the prospects of achievement.

As a leader, unless you have unlimited resources and are operating in a non-competitive environment, productivity and quality improvement initiatives will always be on your agenda. Because they have such a broad influence on company success indicators, improvement in both are panaceas for many problems and challenges. When a company is producing a quality product quickly a lot of good things happen. That is why productivity improvement and enhancing the quality of output are *super processes.*

SUPER PROCESSES

These are the processes that have an exceptionally high impact, good or bad, on the most vital success indicators of a business, such things as costs, sales and profits. Performing super processes well or poorly can make or break a business. Improving productivity and enhancing quality are *super processes.*

A savvy leader puts a high priority on managing *super processes* because they broadly influence so many other things. He also makes certain his employees understand the relationship between these vital processes and the organization's success. Finally, he creates an awareness of the individual employee's role in generating that success and what he gets out of it.

A lot of problems and pressures go away and good things happen when *super processes* are done well. How employees deliver on them is their best bet for a secure future with a strong company.

With *improved productivity*, **companies thrive, customers get better prices, employees get bigger raises, and all is well in the world.** *Enhancing the quality of a product also contributes to this climate of success.* ***Productivity*** **and** *quality* **are the foundations of your organization's good fortune. Don't buy into the myth that you can't have one without the sacrifice of the other. Have them both.**

MANAGEMENT MYTH - 8

To Resolve Issues, You Must Find the Truth

The Reality: *Truth is elusive.*
One person's truth is not another person's truth.

Two people observe the same incident and each builds their own story around it. That is their personal truth, their perspective, and each can be very different. So which one is true? Probably neither. Just like you can't get to fair, you often can't get to "the truth." It is subject to interpretation and tied to reasons, beliefs and perspectives. If you have ever tried to get to the bottom of what really happened when two children have an argument, you know that the truth can be difficult to tie down.

In the business environment, it is prudent to contemplate situations in terms of facts rather than truth. Although the difference between the two are somewhat blurry, truth is interpreted. Facts, on the other hand, are concrete realities more subject to confirmation. When children have an argument, you might not be able to determine the truth about what happened, but a toy was broken and someone

The Truth

has a bump on his head. Those are facts. When dealing with employee issues, there is less opportunity for distortion when you pursue facts rather than the truth. It would take considerable time and effort to get to the truth, and doing so is likely to be an exercise in futility.

> A company policy required employees schedule vacations based on seniority. Young employees complained the older employees whose children were raised took all the prime vacation times, and employees with children had little hope of ever getting a summer or Christmas vacation. Managers reported that because of this policy some of their brightest and best young employees left the company. Others used an exorbitant amount of sick leave during prime vacation times.
>
> Facts derived from the payroll system supported these assertions and the vacation scheduling policy was changed to ensure an even distribution of prime vacation time among all employees. (A company policy that prohibits a parent from sharing vacation and holiday experiences with children is wrong on its face. Yet this policy exists in many companies which illustrates the extent to which practices that don't make sense are engrained in our culture. A savvy leader will challenge them.)
>
> If this change in policy had to be supported at the level of truth, considerable additional effort would be required to determine if the assertions were true and that the policy caused the outcomes. Since it is unlikely parents are going to admit to using sick leave to spend holidays with their children and employees don't always reveal the real reasons

they leave a job, getting to "the truth" is an unlikely proposition. The decision to change the policy was accomplished expeditiously and was based on facts.

Like truth, *intention* is another elusive concept. It can be important in evaluating behavior. Did the person come to the meeting with the intent of disrupting it, or was he just responding to the situation emotionally because of someone else's behavior? Did someone do a good thing because he cared about his team or because of some self-serving motive? Although intent might be important, good luck on figuring that out.

In spite of the illusiveness of intention, it is intriguing. The intent behind someone's actions might cause you to make allowances if the person was well-intended or hard on him if he was not. However, you should have no grand illusions you will ever really know for certain "the truth" about anyone's intentions.

Unless something particularly egregious has happened or the situation is repetitive, the approach in the business world for dealing with truth and intention is the same as what is recommended for managing children who have had an argument. Focus on moving forward.

Leaders must also contend with attitudes, another rather elusive concept. Although attitudes are reflected in behavior and body language, interpretation is required to figure them out. This is why most management training suggests not addressing attitude in appraisals, counseling, and conflict resolution, but rather dealing with specific behaviors, which are more closely tied to facts. That sounds good, but in reality if you can change the attitude, the behavior will follow, and the change will be more permanent. **A change in behavior without a change in attitude may result in compliance for awhile, but the problem is still there.**

> Employees showing up is vital to most operations. When dealing with employees who miss a lot of work or chronically come in late, focusing only on behavior doesn't work well. This is particularly true of young employees new to the work force and accustomed to less intensive school schedules.
>
> A more effective solution is to change their attitude by influencing how they feel and emphasizing their importance to the team and to customers. Not being there is letting customers down and putting a burden on teammates. People are counting on them.
>
> Most likely employees will have feelings of guilt and a sense of failure when they don't show up. Younger employees may have never experienced the alternative feelings realized from being responsible, strong, and disciplined. Drive the behavior through attitude. Suggest they show up every day, even if they don't feel like it, because it means not letting other people down, because it feels good to do the right thing and they are a better person for doing it. Contrast those feelings with the guilt they feel when they stay home.
>
> When they show up for the right personal reasons rather than a demand for behavior, they will experience pride and newfound feelings of being strong, capable, and responsible--a powerful new mental perspective that shifts attitude and delivers the desired behavior.

The Truth

As a practical reality, focusing on both both attitude and behavior is inevitable as they are so closely entwined. Although attitude is more abstract, it is the root cause of behavior and influencing it through inspiration and encouragement yields unquestionable benefits. Refer to behavior in any documentation, but in the process of transforming an employee, leverage the potential of an attitude shift.

CONFLICT AND THE TRUTH: Finding "the truth" in the mist of a conflict is a challenge. Address conflict immediately when it happens. The longer things drag out the more opportunity for distortion. When employees go home at night, they often come back the next day with a whole new story about an incident. Additionally, with time things fester and disrupt the entire operation.

When dealing with conflict issues, talk to each employee separately, but let them know you are going to follow up with a joint discussion. This discourages straying too far from the truth with their individual interpretations. Keep these discussions short, to the point, and information and fact focused. Don't get distracted with decoy issues, emotional drama, or rehashing the past.

Allow employees to save face if feasible. People will say things to justify bad behavior that may not be valid. They may even be ridiculous, but unless it is an egregious situation, letting them save face may help defuse things. If they want to blame their behavior on the fact that their cat died two years ago, consider it entertainment and move on. You may never get to the truth anyway. Focus on getting the behavior you want going forward.

The most important thing is to concentrate on the business issue. Tell them, "Your fighting disrupts the department and our customers don't get their calls answered. This behavior is not okay." Then suggest other ways of reacting.

> If you have two people engaged in constant conflict that disrupts the work force, and you've tried everything, tell them you are going to sit down together with them to hash it out, and if that doesn't work you are going to fire them both. This is clearly a last ditch effort, and you need to have done the leg work necessary to support your action in case you have to execute the threat. However, that is highly unlikely. You may not get to "the truth" about what is going on between them, but odds are, they **will** work it out, at least enough to stop the disruption.

Although there is universally a lot of value placed on the truth, in reality most people look for information that supports what they already believe, ignoring any information that proves otherwise. This makes the truth even more elusive. When you as a leader enlighten employees on the ambiguities of truth and the virtues of factual information and critical thinking, they are much more likely to apply reason and logic to resolving issues rather than arguing about what is "the truth."

A savvy leader maintains a healthy perspective on the elusiveness of truth, intention and attitude and doesn't harbor fantasies about tying them down. He deals with problems by emphasizing hard facts, considering the message he sends to the troops with any reaction, moving forward, and keeping the focus on business issues. The truth may never be known.

MANAGEMENT MYTH - 9

Getting Ahead is All About Who You Know

The Reality: *It is not a good idea to overvalue relationships with superiors. Many a leader has been brought down by subordinates.*

Networking is important, but doing the job you've got well is the real key to advancement. Getting ahead by politicking makes enemies. Earn your success and have the endorsement of others, including peers and subordinates, when you get it. The business world is changing. The "it's who you know" concept is outdated. In today's environment, you have got to deliver.

Don't limit yourself by "managing up," putting your focus on courting superiors, seeking interaction with them, politicking for your next move, and lobbying for endorsement of your opinions while ignoring your peers, subordinates and customers. It will be obvious what you are doing, and it will not sell well. **No one can bring you down quicker than your subordinates. Couple them with a few disenchanted peers and your career is in trouble no matter how much upper management loves you.**

"Managing up" is disrespectful to peers and lower ranked employees. It is arrogant and presumes a superficial superiority. To gain respect, you must give it.

There are leaders who take their coffee cups and saunter into executives' offices, perhaps even the president's, to shoot the bull and lobby for decisions. Unfortunately, they often get them. This means the person making the decision was "used," and at some point he is going to realize that. Since he did not have the input of other stakeholders when he made the decision, it was probably not a good one. Additionally, when others get the ultimatum, usually in an "I got you" moment from the guy doing the lobbying, they are going to be severely disenchanted.

Be in constant contact with your peers and their subordinates, and encourage and require your staff to do the same. If you don't interact with teams and the people actually doing the work, you are eliminating your best chance for a good result. Reach out to everyone. Collaborate with everyone. Visit project team meetings and thank the participants for their work. Tap the talent, seek the input, and reap the benefits of good decisions for all.

This is a matter of respect for others, a basic core value. You cannot be a leader without it. You will simply be a manipulator. **Who are you going to lead if you are too good to interact with the followers?**

You must also guard against being the one manipulated by people who "manage up." When someone comes to you for a decision in a vacuum, send them back to get the perspective of all stakeholders and insist on a joint proposal. Tell them why. Don't let yourself be used by this form of manipulation.

You may think all the power rests in the hands of those running the show. It doesn't. Your subordinates, peers and all their employees have incredible influence, and there are a lot of them. If you decide they are not important, you will STAND OUT, but it will be for all the wrong reasons.

MANAGEMENT MYTH - 10

The Enforcers Are Out to Get You

The Reality: *The enforcers can be your greatest allies.*

The enforcers are the departments in the company and some external organizations that are responsible for assuring everyone complies with requirements. They include, but are not limited to:

Accounting.....assuring compliance with accounting standards, tax codes, budget requirements, expense report criteria, as well as protecting the company's assets.

Human Resources.....enforcing regulatory and legal requirements, protecting the rights and safety of employees, and establishing dress and behavior codes.

Legal.....striving for compliance with laws and regulations and limiting risk.

Quality Control.....ensuring quality products and services.

External Enforcers.....associates from outside the company who conduct audits and reviews. They may be an auditing firm, a regulatory agency, or expert consultants.

Anyone primarily responsible for assuring requirements are met is put in the unfortunate position of being an enforcer. Most everyone resents enforcers, and this provides an opportunity for you, a savvy leader, to STAND OUT and set a new standard for others.

Embrace and engage the enforcers. It is a path to peace of mind because you will have their support and endorsement, and with their help you will comply with requirements and reduce risks. All this is the result of your partnering with them and drawing on their expertise. **If you have integrity, you want to meet all requirements and follow all rules and regulations. The discerning leader sees the enforcers as a mechanism to accomplish that.**

INTERNAL ENFORCERS: What is interesting about internal enforcers is that employees frequently fail to recognize them as members of the same team and instead view them as an intrusive enemy. Their role is protecting, but they are frequently resented for it. Although they are as important to the company's success and viability as any other department, they are almost always under appreciated. This is what provides the perceptive leader with a rare and lucrative opportunity.

> Take advantage of enforcers and their expertise. Be inclusive. Invite them to join your work groups. This prevents re-work, reduces risk, and protects you and your staff from embarrassing mistakes. Don't wait for them to come in on the back end and

derail your efforts because you did not follow a requirement.

Internal enforcers are not out to get you, they are out to help you do the right thing, to ensure your company's success is not sabotaged by someone failing to follow requirements. While protecting the company's reputation, they are also promoting integrity, and they can be the best friend you ever had.

EXTERNAL ENFORCERS: When an enforcer is independent from your company a more arm's length approach is required, but they, too, can be a resource for accomplishment. Even though some are adversarial, you can often find opportunities to benefit from their enforcement efforts. More importantly, treated right, they are likely to become less adversarial.

> A manager of a highly regulated operation was always welcoming and accommodating to auditors. He promoted full disclosure, ensured requests for information were quickly answered and all documents were organized and complete. He also made certain auditors had a comfortable, well-equipped place to work.
>
> If his area was doing something wrong, he wanted to know it, and he would rather auditors find it now than later. He viewed every audit finding as an opportunity to move closer to perfection. He vigorously argued with any findings with which he disagreed, but was receptive and responsive to those that were valid. His staff saw it the same way, and over the years he honed an exceptional operation second to none. His partners in that accomplishment were the auditors.

The Enforcers

Since external auditors perform reviews at many other companies, they are a lucrative and rare source of information on best practices and what is happening in the industry. Your relationship with them determines whether you can tap into that.

Enforcers may regard your inclusion so refreshing and such a novelty that they will become your biggest champions. **They have direct access to the President/CEO, Board of Directors, and other important people. If they think you are exceptional, all the right people are going to know it.**

Everyone wants to be appreciated and respected for the work they do. The enforcers are vital to an organization and they deserve to be valued for their contributions.

When planning and implementing change, let the enforcers in on it and invite their participation in the process. Include them on project teams. Involve them when developing employee training and conducting strategic planning sessions. Invite them to staff meeting and employee events, and have them make presentations to your staff on their areas of expertise. As key players, they are exceptional resources for building your knowledge base and that of all your associates.

Partner with the enforcers. Doing so will set you apart and increase your odds of success.

5 KEYS TO CAREER SUCCESS

KEYS TO SUCCESS - 1

ASPIRATION

A fire in the belly

Aspiration is the primary driver of career accomplishment. It trumps every other attribute an individual brings to the table. When someone aspires to something, they are attuned to exactly what is required to achieve it, and they set out to do those things. Aspiration makes everything else happen, almost automatically. The career path just falls into place.

Successful entrepreneurs and CEOs of companies are rarely the most intelligent employees in their organizations. They are typically not the most educated or credentialed either. What they are is competitive and driven. They *aspire.* As a result, they determine what is required to reach their goals, and then they do those things. It is as simple as that.

People who ascend into the higher ranks of a company do not arrive there by accident. Rarely does someone give them the opportunity out of the blue. They aspired to it and earned it--setting lofty goals, making personal sacrifices and investing hardily in their careers. You could say they have *a fire in the belly*. Those promoting people look for

Aspiration

that fire because they know with it they will get the energy, passion, and commitment required to get the job done.

If you are serious about advancing your career, this *fire in the belly* will come naturally to you. How far you climb will most likely correlate with the intensity of that fire. People rarely achieve things they don't set out to do.

It is important to have an awareness of the fact that not everyone embraces this level of achievement and further to recognize there is nothing wrong with that.

PLATEAUED EMPLOYEES: Not all employees aspire "to get ahead." Also, all employees at some point will reach a plateau where they will not advance any higher whether they want to or not. Corporate American does not deal well with plateaued employees, underestimating their value and awkwardly dancing around their issues. Few companies even acknowledge they exist.

> A leader may have so much enthusiasm for his aspirations that he projects his ambition onto other employees, failing to realize many employees simply want to come to work and earn their pay. They have no interest in advancement. Other employees might want to advance further, but are highly unlikely to do so.
>
> It is not unusual for company leaders to assume all employees want to climb the corporate ladder. Speaking to employees, they rave about opportunities for advancement. This reflects a lack of sensitivity to plateaued employees who resent it when their leaders assume they want what the "go getters" want. It can also stir up desires that will not

Aspiration

be realized for those who plateaued unwillingly. Keep this in mind when speaking to employees.

The definition of success is different for everyone. A person can be successful in their career, but unsuccessful in life. Conversely, a person can be successful at life and not have what most people define as a successful career.

Happiness is not necessarily a synonym for achievement either. Many contented people have modest career aspirations centered around simply providing for their families and focusing on the private aspects of their lives. Where would the organization be without these people? They are company assets. Value them as such.

THE DOWN SIDE OF ASPIRATION: Although aspiration is the primary driver of career success, there is a down side to it. When a person invests too much in achievement, they can lose themselves in it. The imbalance between work and home reeks havoc on one's personal life. Additionally, career competition can overshadow and complicate relationships at work. As a result, an unhealthy detachment sets in. You have probably heard the expression "It is lonely at the top." It can be, if you are so focused on achieving that you miss the people aspects of the work environment.

This is why viewing leadership as *service* to others is so vital. It gives purpose to aspirations. Making a difference for those you lead, your customers, your boss, and everyone around you creates a connectedness which is critical to emotional health and wellbeing.

Therapists counsel many corporate executives and successful entrepreneurs whose identities are closely aligned with accomplishment. When that aspect of their life is threatened, their whole world is in crisis.

Many people become so wrapped up in a certain life style that anything else is viewed as a catastrophe. If you can get past that, there is a sense of strength and freedom in knowing other scenarios can be interesting journeys rather than dreaded disasters.

> After spending many years of intense investment in his career, a man became discouraged and took a break. He quit a lucrative but stressful job in a negative corporate environment, focused on being a student, and painted houses for a living, making just enough money to get by. He was so much happier than when he was working in the high-pressure, high-paying job that when he did stumble across an enticing career opportunity he hesitated to take it.
>
> He did take it, though, and worked as hard as ever but didn't take things as seriously as before. He had a fresh frame of reference. When the company was forced to cut back, everyone was in a panic about the prospect of losing their jobs. There were a lot of negative behaviors and betrayals of loyalties as people clung to their positions at all cost. He, on the other hand, knew something the rest did not. He had a job before he got this one, and he could get another one. He could paint houses and be happy.

There is an infinite supply of career options. The *fire in the belly* may be redirected to a humbler task, but it is always there, smoldering behind a new definition of success.

Most successful people have bounced around in the failure arena at one time or another. It is all part of the journey. Do

Aspiration

not be intimidated by failure. Put that *fire in the belly* to good use no matter what kind of work you are doing. Real success comes from knowing what you do makes a difference for others. Apply your aspiration in a way that it counts for something. Although you may burn out, experience failures, and even take a break from the fire, you will come back stronger than ever because you experienced alternatives and made them count and because you aspire to matter--to make a difference.

A LINE IN THE SAND: As you make your way through the maze of achievement, there will be times when you face the prospect that in order to reach your objectives you must do something you really don't want to do. Maybe you don't want to play golf. Perhaps the required travel interferes too much with your family life. You don't necessarily have to sell yourself out. You may realize your goals anyway, or it may be possible to challenge the requirement and perhaps blaze a trail for others.

> An executive refused to continue to travel in a situation that was dangerous. He suspected that when he took a stand against the requirement his career would be in jeopardy. Instead, other employees who felt the same way but were afraid to buck the system began to speak up and the policy was changed. Consequently, he enjoyed a reputation as a stand up guy.

Some sacrifices will not be worth making. We all have our breakpoints. There will be pressure to do things you don't enjoy. Do them to the extent that they do not impose too much displeasure and angst, but don't be afraid to draw a line in the sand when you feel you are selling yourself out or doing something makes you miserable. Otherwise, you might be successful but mightily unhappy.

If you are serious about career success, articulate clearly in your mind what you want, determine what it takes to accomplish that, and then do those things. Don't lose yourself in the ambition and thereby ignore the potential to matter to others. Aspire so you can *serve*, leave your mark all over your organization, and make the world in which you operate a better place. Aspire so when you look back you will know you made a difference and things are better now because you were there.

KEYS TO SUCCESS - 2

ENDURANCE

*Sometimes we try too hard.
We just need to chill.*

When the going gets tough and you become disenchanted with your job, it is always tempting to solve that problem by going to work for someone else. The occasions worthy of this action are extremely rare. Doing so should be a well-thought-out decision driven by compelling justification. In reality, sticking things out and enduring is often the most viable road to ultimate success.

> An employee was quitting to go to work for another company because he was "tired of the company politics." His boss suggested that if he thought the other company was devoid of politics, he was sorely mistaken. The employee had a good reputation and an obvious career path at his current employer. Who knows what was going to happen to him at the other company. He was convinced to stay, adopted some *coping strategies*, and was eventually promoted to the executive level.

Endurance

A key factor in career success is endurance, and to endure, you need serious *coping strategies*.

JUST CHILL: This is a *coping strategy* where you quit your job in your mind but go to work every day. It is very simply *chilling*. An extremely effective mental perspective, this strategy allows you to pull back and take a break from stress. Amazingly, things will usually smooth out for you after a brief spell of *chilling*.

Surrendering can be the release that gets you through a difficult time. **Sometimes we just try too hard.** *Chilling* is surrendering. When things get tough, the natural inclination is to dig in and fight the good fight, and there are times when that response is appropriate. However, giving up might be the ticket to survival and endurance. Take a break--chill. This is how *chilling* is done:

- Quit your job in your mind but go to work every day.

- Show up at all events and meetings.

- Revise your "To Do" lists. Abandon any projects that are not mandated.

- Do the things required to take care of staff and customers. Focus on nurturing.

- Do as little else as possible.

- Take your coffee cup and tour the building, dropping in to visit other employees.

- Take all your breaks and schedule wonderful lunches. Don't skip any.

- Put in eight hours, no more.

- Enhance the focus on your personal life.

- Don't tell anyone what you are doing. Don't complain about the issues that are distressing you. Just chill.

If you are ambitious, *chilling* will be a strange concept. You are likely to feel guilty about your eight-hour days even though this is how many employees operate all the time. You are not doing anything wrong. You are just coping.

Your increased personal interactions generate support and positive feelings. With your calm state you become very non-threatening and adversaries cool down. Reconnecting with people provides sustenance. The stressful issues work themselves out or lose their importance, and soon you are back in the saddle, stronger than ever, gradually re-starting projects and generating a new "To Do" list.

RECOGNIZE THAT THIS TOO SHALL PASS: It is natural to experience anxiety when the company implements change, particularly when it is an initiative that is well-intended but unlikely to succeed (it happens), or one that has a negative and destructive impact on your area.

As a leader, you will get mandates to do things you know won't work, and you might not be able to convince anyone otherwise. Even though you don't buy into everything your company does, you must comply and give it a good go. For this you need a *coping strategy*. Just tell yourself, "This too shall pass." Remain positive and focus on getting your troops through it. You could be wrong and the outcome may surprise you. At any rate, the transition period will eventually end, and if the program doesn't work, it will eventually go away. Don't get in a wad over it. Just ride it out. *This too shall pass.*

DON'T TAKE ON OTHER PEOPLE'S ISSUES: A great *coping strategy* to avoid stress is to let people own their hang-ups. Don't take them on. They lob something into your court, just let it lie there. Don't pick it up or hit it back unless the incident is truly consequential. Pick your battles so on the rare occasions when you do respond, you are solidly justified and the response is out of character enough to make an impression.

You can't accommodate everyone, not everyone is going to like you, and there are always people who are going to treat you and others poorly because of their own issues. The business world, like high school, is full of bullies. Your focus needs to be on delivering outcomes, serving employees and customers, and nurturing everyone. Don't be distracted from important work by reacting to the behavior of detractors with hang-ups. Save your energy for the important things you are accomplishing.

> A minority employee entering management in the 1970's was treated poorly by others. Things are different today, but at that time a lot of negative behavior surfaced. Unless it was something truly outrageous, the employee ignored it. The way she saw it, they had the problem. She didn't. Her strategy was to ignore bad behavior, avoid confrontations, assume a non-threatening persona, and deliver solid outcomes. She was successful, and those who hassled her in the beginning eventually became her biggest supporters. If she had taken on their issues, the outcome might have been different.

Endurance

Endurance is not always the answer, but rarely is bailing out of a situation the right thing to do. Endurance demonstrates resilience, persistence and perseverance--all redeeming qualities. Don't be the person who every time the going gets tough you "take your marbles and go home." Be the one who prevails against all odds, the tough guy who can take a hit and come out on the other side.

ACTIONS BASED ON PRINCIPLE: Often people will tell you they did something "for the principle of the thing." If you are going to quit a job for the principle of the thing, you are unlikely to achieve a meaningful level of career success. This is why: **There are a lot of principles out there. A few are worth quitting for, most are not.**

If it is a principle worth fighting for, do that, but use prudent judgment. Generally, unless it is an egregious situation, you should not quit. Report it or challenge it if you must, but don't quit. Endure. Once you become more influential you can change things. **You cannot become an agent of change if you quit.**

Another point, principles are not always the result of critical thinking. They are frequently beliefs tied to ideology. Make certain your opinion about the principle is logic based, rational, well thought out, and respectful of other people's rights to their opinions and choices. It is poor judgement to do otherwise.

CONFIDENCE: It is not unusual to become overwhelmed and lose your confidence, especially when taking on a new job. This is the time to endure. *Coping strategies* will help.

-Don't focus on what you don't know. Focus on all that you have learned--how far you have come.

Endurance

-Consider whether anyone else could do it better. Often you can't identify anyone.

-Look at others who are doing something similar. If they can do it, so can you--probably better.

-Look forward to where you will be a year later when you have it whipped and are an expert.

PERSEVERANCE: Endurance implies waiting for the right time and going to the well many times if necessary.

> Employees at a company were expected to be at work every day regardless of weather. Icy or snowbound roads were no excuse for not showing up or being late. If they did not comply, they were penalized through attendance policies and a glaring boss when they did show up. Consequently, on bad weather days employees loaded kids into cars and drove on treacherous roads to deliver them to caretakers, or they left them at home unsupervised.
>
> One of the company executives almost had a car accident one day when a woman with an infant in the car slid toward her at an icy intersection. It occurred to her there was something inherently wrong with a business culture that puts families at risk like that. She immediately changed the practices in her area of responsibility.
>
> She softened enforcement of the attendance policy, installed flex hours for bad weather days, opened the office on evenings and weekends so employees could make up lost time, and stopped the intimidation and monitoring of arrival times. However, it took her eight years to get a company-

Endurance

> wide change of attendance policy. Time after time she proposed it and eventually made it happen because she persevered.

There are a lot of practices and customs in institutions that don't make sense. They are ingrained and not easily changed. Most people don't think about challenging them. When you do, and if you do it often, people may be puzzled by your tenacity. However, if it makes sense, most likely you will eventually prevail.

> In spite of the fact that business is compelled to do quarterly reporting because of long-running Wall Street requirements, an executive noted that many reports and costly meetings could be done just two or three times a year. This reduced the cost and time invested in preparing and delivering reports by at least one-fourth, a substantial savings. This change also put these reports off-cycle of the required quarterly reports, an added benefit.

When challenging something ingrained in the culture of a company and ultimately prevailing, you leave a legacy. That is *service*.

BE NON-THREATENING: With a *fire in your belly*, you may be perceived as a threat to those competing for promotions, even to higher ranking executives who see you as competition if you enter their ranks. On the other end of the spectrum, non-competitors may resent your success.

This suggests that a low-key persona is appropriate--a frame of mind of *quiet confidence*. Don't toot your own horn and broadcast your successes. Let the outcomes speak for themselves. Use moderation in cheerleading and championing your employees. Amazingly, other leaders may interpret such praise as you suggesting your staff is better than theirs. They may be, but nothing is accomplished by broadcasting it.

Don't be vocal about your aspirations. Even in interviews for promotions it is best to exude a non-threatening image. Definitely act interested, but the commonly proposed recommendation that you suggest you want the interviewer's job is not a good one. He might be plateaued and planning to keep it for a long time, or he may see an ambitious rising hot shot as competition for his next move. Remember, everything is a balancing act. You can do too much or too little of anything. Be savvy. Walk the line.

LAY LOW: When political power changes and you find yourself on the down side of the new power brokers, don't quit. Simply *lay low*. Don't hold any ground. Be prepared to adjust and sacrifice. Avoid gossip and don't take part in any circling of the wagons. Simply follow all instructions, meet all requirements, and make yourself as invisible as possible. Keep doing your job and delivering the best outcomes possible without rocking the boat. The winds of political bias are amazingly fluid. You might find yourself in the winning camp if you simply *endure*.

If you aspire to a serious career, *endurance* will be a key factor in achieving that goal. Being resilient and not quitting when others would affords you an opportunity to ultimately gain influence and become a change agent. The rewards of hanging in there can be enormous, and they will have happened because you endured.

KEYS TO SUCCESS - 3

Doing What Is Required
AND THEN SOME

Don't settle for mediocrity.

As you climb the corporate ladder, there are fewer positions and a whole lot of people wanting them. Acknowledge this reality and face it head on with actions that ensure you STAND OUT from the mass of aspiring achievers. Just doing your job and doing it well is not enough. Leave no stone unturned when seeking that edge. To compete you have to do what is required AND THEN SOME.

BE EXTRAORDINARY: Look for an unpopular project or problem everyone else avoids because they believe it can't be done, it is too much work, or it will stir things up too much. Make certain it is one that plays to your strengths, then take it on. Ask your staff to do the same. Do this over and over, and you and your employees will STAND OUT.

By doing this, you and your team model leadership behavior that makes the entire organization stronger. Demonstrating courage and initiative, fearlessly attacking long-running problems, and refusing to accept mediocrity inspire the same from others and everyone wins.

BUILD AN EXTRAORDINARY STAFF: Do not settle for mediocrity, for yourself or others on your team. Require commitment, initiative, work ethic, courage, and fortitude. Work gets done through people. Invest in your people. Put people first. Set high standards. Role model work ethic.

> You cannot accept mediocrity from a management employee. A non-management employee might get by with just barely delivering, doing their job, meeting standard, and nothing more. However, when a management person behaves this way, you will always be at odds with him. **You can't get to extraordinary without an exceptional leadership team.**

When interviewing job applicants, be very clear about the required work ethic and the demands of the job. It is not unreasonable to expect leaders to go the extra mile, and they should do so willingly. Once your expectations are known, slackers will lose interest in the position. Go getters will be enthused. Take the final applicants to lunch before making an offer. Things will show up that were not obvious in the interview, both good and bad.

MATCH THEM UP: Become an expert at matching employee skill sets and innate abilities to the work at hand. This will require you and your staff learn how to identify innate qualities in people and to understand the work processes compatible with their talent. Mismatched employees struggle, are not happy, and cannot get to extraordinary which makes it difficult for you to deliver the AND THEN SOME.

SET LOFTY GOALS: You will never get to be number one if you don't aspire to be number one. Set safe, mediocre goals and you will get mediocre results. Slow and steady progress has its place, but the savvy leader presses for momentum--that acceleration that optimizes progress. He seeks *exponential synergy.* Set your sights high and back them up with actions.

> When a manager informed the president of his organization that he had a plan to be number one in the country in a ranking where the company had meandered around the midpoint for years, the president was shocked. No one had ever even thought about aspiring to that level of success. It took a couple of years, but the firm eventually made it to the number one slot. It was an outrageous objective, and an accomplishment that would have never happened if the leader had not set that goal.

MAXIMIZE SUPER PROCESSES: Identify *super processes,* the ones that have the most significant impact on the company's most vital success indicators such as costs, sales, and profitability. Focus on improving these processes to ensure maximum return on the investment of team resources. **A lot of good things happen when *super processes* are enhanced and vital success indicators improved.** Following are three *super processes* common to most companies:

> **PRODUCTIVITY IMPROVEMENT:** This typically has a broad impact on outcomes for most every organization and department in a company and is easily labeled a *super process* deserving of intense focus. Improving productivity means you can do more with less, budget problems go away, less time is spent hiring and training even though the company is growing,

employees will be more successful, there is more money to go around, prices are lower and customers are happier.

IMPROVING QUALITY: Every associate in the company is responsible for producing a quality product and serving the customer, even if they never interact with one directly. Behind-the-scenes people serve the customer through their support of other employees. All employees are "keeping the promise." Improving the quality of products and services is a *super process* that affects sales and customer satisfaction, prevents re-work, and enhances the company's image.

EMPLOYEE DEVELOPMENT: This is a *super process,* primarily because it impacts *employee loyalty* which has far-reaching implications. (More about that later.) Probably nothing else you do will have a more significant exponential or synergetic influence on outcomes than employee development. Time and money invested in learning pays huge dividends.

To maximize the potential of *super processes,* focus on them when doing both long-term strategic planning and when determining daily priorities. Set specific objectives to improve them, and follow up with tactical actions to make that happen. Measure and report the results.

**It is easy to get distracted by mandated projects, paperwork, and fire fighting and not invest energy and resources in what really counts. Savvy leaders know what really counts--the *super processes.*

INDISPENSABLE EMPLOYEES: All knowledge should be redundant. Any dependency on a single person puts your company at risk. People who make themselves indispensable are often intimidating. Require they share their knowledge. Implement processes to ensure that happens and monitor and follow-up as necessary. You are accountable for ensuring *depth of knowledge* in your area.

This applies to yourself, as well. The prospect of you realizing a promotion rests on someone being ready to take your place. Always be grooming several candidates to replace you. Don't pre-judge which one might ultimately prevail. You might be surprised. **Make yourself valuable but don't make yourself indispensable.**

SUCCESSION PLANNING: You are also responsible for *succession planning* and assuring an appropriate *depth of human resources* in your departments. Many leaders neglect this. That is what makes it an AND THEN SOME when you do it. It does not have to be a major, formal project. Simply target and groom employees for future vacancies, and have at least one person ready to take everyone's place, preferably more. **Be gracious when the wonderful employees you develop find opportunities in other divisions. Your supplying top-of-the-line employees to other areas enhances your reputation as an expert at identifying and developing human resources, and those people you developed and nurtured will increase your connections and influence in other divisions.**

PLAY TO YOUR STRENGTHS: Seek positions and projects that fit your talents and for which you have a passion. Your being preoccupied with numerous projects that you selected may keep you from being assigned others that don't match your skill set.

BE A CHANGE AGENT: Be the person who initiates change, who transforms the organization. Challenge established customs and practices that no longer fit the times. Embrace fresh ideas, introduce pilot programs, and explore unique approaches. Turn you staff loose with out-of-the-box brainstorming, experiments and trials. Give them credit when they are successful. Be the architect of progress and leave your mark all over the company.

On the other hand, remember that you can do too much or too little of anything. Some practices are tried and true and timeless. Don't be so focused on progress and innovation that you abandon the time-tested, proven basics.

POWER BROKER: Be the "go to" person for influencing decisions and getting things done, the one who forms liaisons horizontally and vertically, who has the influence to remove barriers and who champions action. Build connections and establish relationships with industry leaders, governing agencies, and those upon whom you depend to run your operation. **Look for ways to use these connections to connect people to each other.**

VOLUNTEER: Participate actively in company and industry social and charity events. Serve on committees and task forces and encourage your staff to do the same.

TAKE ADVANTAGE OF IMAGE: Don't clutter up potential advancement prospects with how you look. Dress for the job you want, not the one you've got. **It is important that those making promotion decisions can visualize you at their level.** Remember you are competing against other candidates. Any little thing could turn the tide when the promotion decision is made. Don't follow the masses. Look like the serious, confident employee you are.

Your image can be the AND THEN SOME that makes a difference. **Brand yourself through your image.**

HAVE AN OWNER PERSPECTIVE: Manage your operation like you own it, like it is your personal money being spent and you must generate profits to support your family. If you were running your own company, you would never inflate a budget or distort information because you would want to know what the real numbers are. You would avoid waste, ferret out inefficiencies, and seek optimal outcomes. It is easy to slip into organizational pitfalls and lose sight of your fiduciary responsibility as a leader. Don't do it. **Run your operation like a business--your business.**

DO THE RIGHT THING, EVEN IF IT HURTS: Here is an example of a tough call that is the right thing to do, but one that entails significant sacrifice.

> For years everyone at a company ignored budgeting requirements and padded their budgets big time. The philosophy was, if you don't get it and spend it this year, you won't get it next year. (It may be appropriate to build some cushion into the budget for contingencies, but this was excessive and not done with full disclosure.)
>
> The budget increased exponentially every year, even when sales and revenues were down. Those doing the padding had the benefit of never having to explain budget overages, and they received incentives for coming in under budget. Not being real, the budgets encouraged waste and discouraged pursuing efficiencies. Certainly no efficiency gains were factored into the budget at a realistic level.

What if you submitted a "real" budget, even if you are the only one to do so? Here is the challenge. Without the excessive padding, you will most likely have overages to explain. Because salary is tied to budget performance, personal incomes may be reduced. You have incorporated efficiency gains from initiatives into your budget that might not materialize. In hard times when everyone has to cut back, you don't have the padding others have. Your staff will not have the same advantages as their peers, and everyone in the company will think you're an idiot.

All of this suggests a huge downside, but there is an upside. You will earn a reputation among the finance staff and upper management for following requirements, even when it hurts. You will be acting with integrity. You will manage your operation like you owned it, you will know what the real numbers are, and you will have your self-respect. Most importantly, you will STAND OUT.

No doubt you can refuse to comply with some requirements and still climb the corporate ladder. After all, everyone is doing it. The question is, how do you want to get to the top? Maybe you want to do that by being extraordinary, by doing the AND THEN SOME, and by doing the right thing.

KEYS TO SUCCESS - 4

A Learning Environment

*The road to employee loyalty
is through investing in learning.*

As a leader, you create the work environment. A vital component of doing that is ensuring *a learning environment.* **Rarely will you find an opportunity with the potential to yield a larger return on investment than people learning. Knowledge gained is applied over the immense span of careers, and *employee loyalty* generated from a learning environment has sweeping implications. Invest in learning, and you will realizes impressive returns.** To make this investment, you must do things few leaders do. Make employee learning an absolute top priority, and invest in it hardily. Here is how to do that.

PERSONAL INVOLVEMENT: Others leaders may be mentoring a few people, but learning is most likely not at the top of their priority list, and it is unlikely they are personally delivering learning to their employees. You want to STAND OUT? **Personally invest the time and effort to ensure every employee in your division is always learning. Be hands on and participate in their learning.**

A Learning Environment

It is rare for a corporate executive to conduct training. They might introduce the session, endorse it and encourage it, but unless it is mandated, they are unlikely to execute it. That is a missed opportunity.

> A senior executive volunteered to teach supervisor training classes for his company. The director of training called to suggest a class be cancelled because there were only three people signed up. The executive insisted on doing it anyway saying, "Three supervisors doing a better job makes a difference for sixty employees and a countless number of customers all day every day. My facilitating that effort may be the most important work I do all week."

The value of your personal involvement in learning is huge, and it is a generous way of sharing and serving others.

SHARING KNOWLEDGE

Set a goal that everyone on your leadership team knows everything you know. Personally deliver knowledge. Require that every leader in your area is learning and sharing what he learns. In addition, provide learning opportunities for all employees, no matter their rank. When everyone is learning and broadly sharing knowledge, *a learning environment* is created.

SHARE THE LEARNING: Have a meeting once a month where the management staff and peer leaders in your division gather in a meeting room, perhaps with brown bag lunches, and share with each other everything learned

A Learning Environment

during the month as well as knowledge from years of education and experience. **The goal is: Everyone knows what everyone else knows.**

Even though attendance is voluntary, these sessions can be so valuable that employees will enthusiastically give up their lunch hour, and they will not want to leave. They will even schedule their vacations around these meetings.

During the month, jot down notes every time you learn something. Encourage your staff to do the same. Then pass these *lessons learned* on to your team at the monthly meeting. Produce handouts on key points, distribute articles, and provide summaries of books and seminars. Document the most important information on-line to share with future leaders.

Work gets done through people. These information sharing meetings yield a high caliber of staff. Reputations flourish. Employees become experts in the know, and your company becomes rich with exceptional human resources. Here are examples of information and knowledge to share with your leaders in the course of a year:

- During budget season, do a session on accruals, depreciation, fixed and variable costs and other accounting and economic principles.

- When company financial statements come out, instruct staff on how to interpret them, how the ratios are calculated, and what they say about the company.

- When the annual report is issued, go over the key points. Emphasize company core values, mission, and goals. Relate them to what is being done in the employees' departments.

A Learning Environment

- During planning season, train on strategic and tactical planning, threats and opportunities, brainstorming techniques, goal setting, and goal translation.

- When the company makes acquisitions and procurements, review the analysis processes and decision factors.

- During appraisal season, train on job descriptions, performance evaluations, coaching, counseling, documentation, interviewing, hiring and firing.

- Develop a document on when, how and what to report to a superior and how to go beyond that if necessary.

- If you are involved in any legal or regulatory situations, share everything you learned in that regard. Provide feedback on audits. Ask the team to strategize on how to avoid legal cases and audit findings in the future.

- Report experiences of task forces and committees. Share information on how project teams are managed and how to be good project leaders and followers.

- Provide updates on current political activities and regulatory actions important to your industry.

- Have staff share success stories, optimal ways of doing things, and lessons learned on the job.

- When an employee reads a book, experiences a seminar or some other learning opportunity, have them share the highlights.

- Invite people from other departments to talk about what their area does and important initiatives underway.

- Share information coming out of the public relations department. Equip employees to talk to friends and relatives about company and industry issues--to be public relations representatives. In addition to creating a deeper awareness of the company, this builds pride and a feeling of being a part of something larger than oneself.

Imagine the sweeping impact of all this knowledge, and it is just the tip of the iceberg. Over the course of a year, a virtual wealth of knowledge will be shared and manuals of proven methods and best practices generated. Information will be flying. Staff will get experience speaking in front of a group in a safe, friendly environment. Enlightenment and awareness will shoot through the ceiling, and employees will eat it up. If this much progress is made in a year, imagine the power of learning over the years.

People from other departments will notice all this progress and ask to attend your meetings. Include them and encourage them to spin off meetings in their areas. **Ask your leaders to set up their own *share the learning* luncheons with their employees.** Imagine the impact of top performers in departments giving hints and tips to other employees. This is a *learning environment*.

PERSONAL DEVELOPMENT PLANS: A learning environment includes everyone. It means a lot to employees when their leaders demonstrate they care enough to invest in them. Have a personal development plan for every employee each year. Otherwise, employee development gets put on the back burner.

A learning environment requires educational opportunities-- classes and programs to support learning. Most of the training can be done in-house with existing resources by putting together an in-house curriculum on two levels.

IN-HOUSE CURRICULUM

> **LEVEL I:** A mandated course each year for every employee on a global company topic, such as core values, integrity and ethics, diversity, coping with change, industry or company issues, or quality.
>
> **LEVEL II:** Optional courses on more specific topics, such as team building, stress management, consensus building, project management, writing skills, EI, or peer leadership.
>
> Every employee gets Level I training. Level II can be different for each employee based on need and interest. Let each employee participate in determining what Level II development he will experience. These do not have to be long involved sessions. They can be all day or a few hours, perhaps with part of the training on line. That is a small investment to make to realize a huge return of employee loyalty and learning.

If your company has a training department, you can usually engage them in facilitating training for your staff, or you can do it with your leadership team. This is an opportunity for them to polish their presentation skills. If they are looking to do the AND THEN SOME, they will volunteer to conduct training. **Always be engaged in teaching something yourself.**

SEMINARS AND COURSES: There are a broad range of costs associated with external learning opportunities, but inexpensive ones are out there. Investing a couple of hundred dollars a year in an employee for a seminar, particularly for your leadership staff, is worthwhile. Community college courses are generally inexpensive and classes are on the employee's own time. Over and above the learning, the message sent to employees when you underwrite their learning makes it a worthy investment. The return is *employee loyalty*.

BUDDY UP PROGRAM: Management staff, especially front line supervisors, are preoccupied with the day-to-day running of operations and often fail to network adequately. A formal "Buddy Up Program" where team leaders are matched up for a one-on-one lunch once a week creates alliances and learning. Rotate buddies every month or two. Ask employees to report what they learned from each other at the monthly leadership meetings.

BUILD ON STRENGTHS: There is controversy over whether to focus employee development on eliminating weaknesses or building on a person's strengths. Don't ignore weaknesses, but there are limits to the extent of potential improvement realized by focusing on them, and they require considerable effort.

On the other hand, developing strength in the area of an employee's innate capabilities requires less effort, offers more prospect of success and the employee is happier focusing on their positive attributes. Think about what it was like in school when you were in a class you hated contrasted with one you enjoyed. You must strike a balance here. Some weaknesses need to be overcome, but play to a person's strengths when targeting learning experiences and watch them soar.

A Learning Environment

Creating a learning environment and developing employees to the extent suggested here fires everyone up and turns them loose. All you have to do is let the teams work. With the knowledge and confidence you have given them through all this learning, you will have a powerhouse of a team.

Learning is a *super process* that creates and sustains *employee loyalty* which, in turn, influences turnover, production, morale, and a host of other important outcomes. In spite of the fact that loyalty is a bit elusive when it comes to measurement, it is a key success indicator in any operation. Making it a priority generates dividends all over the place.

Put learning at the top of your agenda. Engage your leadership team in developing and conducting learning opportunities. Most importantly, personally share what you know and what you learn. Give employees the gift of knowledge and awareness. The results are expansive, and employees benefit both professionally and personally from these growth experiences. Create a learning environment. Do it so you STAND OUT, and do it because leadership is nurturing and *serving* others.

KEYS TO SUCCESS - 5

Become an Expert In Your Industry and In Business

Perhaps you can fake it till you make it, but why not get all over it and just make it?

You can't be a competent high-ranking executive in a company if you are not an expert in the industry and in business. The key word here is "competent." We all know incompetent people who achieve executive status, usually riding someone's coat tails. Don't be that person.

If you don't thoroughly understand how your industry is regulated, its products, competition, and place in the scheme of business, you cannot be an effective leader. Further, if you don't understand the basic fundamentals of business, you are going to make some bad decisions and look foolish in the process. To advance in your career you need to get on the learning track big time, not necessarily in the traditional educational forums. That can take too long. You must pursue every avenue possible to learn quickly.

> An executive read that if a person spent 30 minutes a day studying something, they would be an expert in a year. As a result, he spent many lunch hours

reviewing reading material that crossed his desk which he ordinarily would not have taken time to read. He soon became an expert on his industry and several related ones. He was constantly amazed at how often he was able to apply the information he learned. Then, he passed all this learning on to his staff, and they became experts. In today's environment you could spend thirty minutes a day on-line and easily find enough industry information to achieve expert status in a year.

When a person first starts studying something, a lot of the information is confusing and overwhelming, but learning builds on itself. As more information is acquired, old information becomes more clear. Soon the person can read a complex industry article and understand all of it. He is an expert.

BUSINESS FUNDAMENTALS: It is astounding how many people with a business degree move up in a company and don't apply the basic fundamentals of business.

> An executive refused to support acquiring a new system. His position was the company hadn't gotten their money's worth out of their investment in the old one. Since the old system was inhibiting production and producing poor output costing the company customers and huge amounts of sales revenue every year, his logic was seriously flawed.
>
> The cost of the original system was a **sunk cost,** as defined by a basic economic principle. It makes no economic sense to continue doing something into the future just because you spent money on it in the past. It is the look forward that matters. Cut your losses and get the optimal future outcome.

In another case, an executive required all his departments cut costs equally across the board. This forced an area to cut staff that resulted in a significant negative effect on sales and revenue far exceeding any cost savings and drove up costs in other departments.

In another instance, a company dissolved a division because it was not profitable. However, it was covering 30% of the company's fixed costs which after the dissolution created losses in other divisions who had to pick up the 30%. Also, the dissolved division had operated in a key market area that gave the company influence vital to other divisions, and that was lost as well.

As a savvy leader, you do not want to be responsible for such oversights. If you don't understand the concepts of sunk costs, fixed costs, variable costs, opportunity costs, overhead, depreciation, accruals, cash flow, return on investment, use of capital and all the other basic concepts of finance, economics, accounting, and statistics you need to put yourself on a steep learning curve.

Every leader, no matter what department he is in, has functional responsibilities that involve business fundamentals. This is not as intimidating as it seems. You don't have to take a college course. With a computer or books from a college book store, you can learn what you need to know on a topic in a couple of weeks. Do it. Map out a plan of learning and go after it. Become an expert.

BUSINESS LAW: Another important subject a savvy leader should be knowledgeable about is business law. Not grasping these basic concepts can cause you to put your company and yourself at risk and reveal to others you are woefully unaware of basic business acumen.

PUBLIC SPEAKING: It is vital to be a good speaker if you are to be an effective leader. **The best way to learn to speak is to speak.** When you are talking about something for which you have a passion and on which you are an expert, you will do a good job. Your being an effective speaker is a gift to others.

> Someone asked a speaker if he was nervous when he spoke. He responded that there was always some anxiety, but very little because he focused not on himself and whether he was doing a good job, but rather on the audience and whether they were getting what they needed. He said, "It is not about me. It is about them. Giving them what they need and making it interesting and enjoyable gets me outside of myself."

You owe it to yourself and your staff to be a good communicator and to ensure all your leaders are as well. Start a speaking club in your organization where employees have lunch together and critique each other's presentations (real ones), or bring Toastmasters in-house. Creating outstanding speakers adds a new dimension to the caliber of human resources in your organization.

WRITING: Experts write well, with political correctness, objectivity, assertiveness as opposed to aggression, without emotion and always sticking to the facts. Anything put in writing is out there for everyone to see. Because of the enduring nature of the written word, it is probably the most visible thing a leader can do. **Put something in a memo or on-line that is unpleasant enough to be entertaining and odds are everyone is going to see it.**

PERSPECTIVE CHECK

Read everything you are about to publish over and over, each time wearing a different hat. Mentally take on different perspectives of key people--the president, your boss, the customer, employees, a lawyer, anyone who might challenge the information or be hurt or insulted by it, and your mother. When contemplating how others interpret your message and the outcomes of their interpretations, you will re-write.

When writing, don't have as an objective to make someone look bad. As much as possible, allow people to save face. Focus on facts and potential solutions. It is less important to prove you are right or that someone else is wrong than to simply get the best outcome you can get. **If you have axes to grind, don't do it on paper or online.**

PROJECT MANAGEMENT: Every leader needs project management skills, as does his staff. **As part of a learning environment every leader and those being groomed for leadership should be leading at least one project at all times.** A lot of work and learning gets done when employees hone project management skills by actually managing projects. Progress is exponential.

PROJECT MODEL

Have a team develop a best practices document on how to manage a project, so both team leaders and participants know how to be good leaders and followers. A document on requirements for running projects delivers a huge return on

investment through the synergy generated from teams efficiently administering and completing projects. Make certain to follow the model requirements yourself.

STRATEGIC PLANNING: Planning is the foundation of progress, so it is crucial that leaders are experts at it. Whether it is required or not, you need a plan for your area of responsibility every year. Learn how to do it well, and do it with at least a five-year outlook.

Include in the planning process key people from the enforcers and areas that support your department. Then develop concrete action plans to realize that plan. This is where you define objectives, establish priorities, set specific measurable goals, develop tactical steps to accomplish them, and assign projects. **Broadly disseminated the plan in your departments, to those areas supporting you and, of course, to your boss.**

Planning is the path to assuring the big picture is not overlooked and top priorities are addressed. It is a key to getting upper management approval for your initiatives and to soliciting support from those upon whom you depend to realize them. The plan will be your guide as you progress through the year and a mechanism through which to inspire action and measure results. Without a plan, you are severely handicapped. **A savvy leader always has a plan.**

HUMAN DYNAMICS: You and your staff need to be experts on team building, matching employees' talents to work, inspiring commitment and work ethic, interpreting customer needs, and a whole host of other people factors related to your business. Include an abundance of human dynamics programs in your learning and development plans so you can leverage the wisdom, talent, power and potential of people and so you can nurture them effectively.

CRITICAL THINKING: Good decisions are the product of knowledge and prudent judgment wisely applied. Rational interpretations, analytical expertise, and logical thought processes are imperative to realizing exceptional outcomes. Become knowledgeable on critical thinking processes. These, combined with your intuition, will make you a sophisticated, savvy decision maker. You will not be perceived as an expert if you are not applying logic and rational thought to your thinking. College courses are available on critical thinking, but one or two good books will give you what you need.

Logical, rational thinking requires a clear head, clarity of direction, and relevant focus.

> When in the depths of a conglomeration of daily events at the office, the mind can become overwhelmed, clouded, and sluggish. This affects critical thinking. You can become so immersed in details that you lose sight of the big picture and creative thinking is stymied. There is an easy solution: exercise. Walk on your lunch hour or break and your brain will suddenly let loose of all the clutter. Tactics, solutions and creative ideas will present themselves abundantly.

CHURNING: This is an example of a lack of critical thinking. Every method for accomplishing work or structuring an organization has pros and cons. While operating under one method or structure, people notice the cons associated with it. They often ignore the pros since they are focused on the problems. To resolve them, they convert to the other method or structure without considering the pros and cons of both options. The outcome is the trading of one set of problems for another and, worse yet, going through a disruptive transition to do it.

> A company had a *decentralized* organizational structure which presented problems with monitoring, controlling, communications, and costs of having facilities in various locations. They solved those problems by *centralizing* and then began experiencing the negatives of that structure which were a lack of representation in their customer areas, high metropolitan labor costs, and capacity issues in their building. Upon investigation, it was discovered that approximately every seven years in the history of this venerable organization a switch was made to or from centralization.

This is churning. It is often the result of a new, ambitious executive rushing to make his mark by doing something spectacular. As you select projects with the objective of standing out, do the research. Churning is disruptive and wasteful. Application of critical thinking techniques and comprehensive cost/benefit analysis can stop the madness.

When you don't understand something at work, seek a source and learn. Become an expert. Participate in the learning environment you champion for others. When you and your team become experts on your industry, business fundamentals, and human dynamics, you create a strong organization, one that is a model for human resource development. Your becoming an expert postures you to be of *service* to others and to leave your mark all over your organization and industry.

SUMMARY - THE SAVVY LEADER

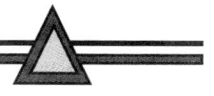

What does *The Savvy Leader* look like? When he walks into a room his appearance says he is serious. He has an air of self-assurance about him--quiet confidence. He is not boastful or arrogant. Grounded in core values, he knows he is a person of integrity and purpose, and he requires the same of others. People look at him and think, "I want what he has."

He is an expert at what he does, never stops learning, and ensures his staff does the same. He has a fire in his belly, but he doesn't broadcast it, and he respects and admires those who have chosen another path.

Recognizing work gets done through people, he invests in them and considers facilitating their work and learning as an absolute top priority.

He refuses to be a victim and goes for the win. When something fails, he focuses on the rally and the next opportunity to win, and he takes everyone else along for the ride.

He is a logical, rational thinker who is not afraid to waver when information suggests it. He expects a lot, holds himself and others accountable and stands ready to support them in that endeavor. Celebrating the accomplishments of others, he is generous with recognition and appreciation.

Summary - The Savvy Leader

A prudent risk taker, he proactively attacks problems and fearlessly embraces change. Tenacious and determined, he is astutely watchful for the right moment to make his move and is fearless in making it because he has made himself an expert. He is a valuable asset to the organization, and he knows it because he has left his mark all over it.

He is a stand up guy, accepting full accountability and insisting on it from others. He fits in, but he also stands out. He is his own person with his own unique style. He recognizes that everything is a balancing act, that you can do too much or too little of anything.

The savvy leader understands the importance of establishing a hierarchy of priorities upon which to base decisions. The customer is always at the top of this list. He knows that what is best for them is best for everybody. He focuses attention on super processes and applies resources where they really count.

He creates the context in which everyone functions, a framework for behavior expressed in terms of core values, vision, mission, and purpose. He plans, communicates, and inspires. He nurtures everyone, including himself. A team player, he is both a good leader and a good follower.

He views his role as a leader as one of service, and he dedicates himself to making a difference. **When adversity happens, he responds in a way that when it passes he can say things went better for others because he was there.**

You can become this person. You simply have to decide to do it. Here are some things to think about as you take that journey:

Summary - The Savvy Leader

A sense of your personal core values and striving every day to live by them provide you a depth of character and inner strength to do amazing things. Your being grounded in these values will shine through to others.

As you learn, leadership gets easier, gentler, more natural, and you begin to feel you are doing what you were born to do. It doesn't get any better than that.

As life happens, be prepared to stay the course or embrace change, whichever seems appropriate in the moment. Face challenges with the objective of making it better because you were there, whether as a leader or a follower. Later, when you look back at these challenges, you will know you mattered.

Finally, step up. Be fearless and courageous. Take on the things others avoid while picking your challenges wisely to take full advantage of your talents.

You came into this world with your own special, unique set of innate capabilities. They are a gift you received at birth, your own personal magic. Don't waste them. Re-gift. Not everyone does that. When you do it you will stand out, you will matter, and you will nurture and serve those you lead and those you follow because you know that leadership is *service*.

APPENDIX

---SAMPLE---

CORE VALUES

INTEGRITY.....is being trustworthy, forthright and honorable, keeping your word, and behaving in an ethical, principled manner in all areas.

DUTY.....is having the courage to be a stand up person, the fortitude to rally and persist, meet obligations, carry your share of the load and make personal sacrifices for the good of the whole.

ENCOURAGEMENT.....is being mindful of the human dignity every person deserves, showing consideration and regard for all persons and creating an environment of purpose and cooperation.

ACCOUNTABILITY.....is a willingness to acknowledge responsibility, to be answerable for decisions and all related implications, taking ownership and striving to make things better.

SEEKING.....is being on a constant quest for improvement, progress, creative solutions, knowledge and personal growth.

APPENDIX (con't)

--- SAMPLE ---

BEHAVIORAL MODEL

The core values of the company are what our organization is about. This behavioral model, developed by employees, reflects how to express those values. All personnel are expected to be staunch defenders of these core values and to adopt, promote, and demonstrate them as a condition of employment.

INTEGRITY:
Be trustworthy, loyal, truthful, forthright and ethical.
Meet deadlines and keep promises.
Follow all laws, policies, and regulations.
Report accurately and with full disclosure.
Require of yourself what you require of others.

DUTY:
Meet obligations and pull your weight.
Willingly sacrifice for the good of the whole.
Show up, be on time, and participate.
Be steady, sure, focused and positive.
Be a team player, a good leader and follower.

Encouragement:
Support all associates and facilitate their work.
Help everyone be the best they can be.
Treat everyone with dignity and respect.
Honor people's differences and personal choices.
Rally others to meet challenges and to persevere.

Accountability:
Take full responsibility for outcomes.
Accept responsibility for personal behavior.
Fulfill personal and business obligations.
When something is not happening right, fix it.
Champion proactive problem prevention.

Seek:
Search for progressive ideas and creative solutions.
Strive to improve efficiency and outcomes.
Pursue lofty goals and grand achievements.
Engage with others in the quest for progress.
Embrace learning, knowledge, and personal growth.

INDEX
of
BEST PRACTICES

This list of *best practices* characterizes a package of concrete actions designed to orchestrate your success at becoming a *savvy leader*. Further, they have the potential to transform your organization through the influence of its leaders.

Although it cannot be guaranteed that all the proposed practices are applicable to every reader's environment, they are the product of applied leadership and have been proven in real business settings. Your judgment can guide you on their adaptability to the unique characteristics of your own situation. In those instances where they do not fit, they still have value in that they are worthy of reflection and deliberation as you develop your own formula for leadership success.

Target the *high priority/easy to do* practices and those that deliver the biggest return on investment of time and effort and implement them. Then, take it to another level and install more. With each wave more exponential synergy kicks in. Your company will flourish. You, those you lead, and those you follow will all stand out. You will be savvy leaders who deliver results that count. You will make a difference. You will matter, and you will *serve*.

BEST PRACTICES

INTEGRITY GAPS.....Find them and get rid of them. Stop saying it or stop doing it. p. 14

CORE VALUES.....Adopt core values for your department. Live by them and require everyone else do the same. p. 16

BEHAVIORAL MODEL.....Adopt a list of behaviors to support the core values and require everyone live by them. p. 17

EVERYONE LEADS.....Recognize that everyone leads and tap into that. p. 19

PEER LEADERS.....Empower steady employees making them ambassadors, advocates, advisors and credible messengers. Buddy them up with new employees. p. 20

ACCOUNTABILITY....Apply accountability broadly. Don't stop at reasons and excuses. p. 23

EXCUSES AND REASONS.....Never give or accept a report that stops at reasons and excuses. Require root causes analysis, prevention and management accountability. p. 23

DO SOMETHING MANAGEMENT.....You see a problem, own it, fix it, be all over it. If not you, who? p.24

ROOT CAUSE AND PREVENTION.....Find the root cause of all problems. Seek prevention. Don't confuse symptoms with root causes. p. 24

Index of Best Practices

REPORTING.....Direct reports must report. Establish routine reporting requirements for your staff and yourself. p. 26

RESCUES.....When someone is always rescuing, seek out the root cause of the problem so the rescue is no longer necessary. p. 26

DEPENDENCIES.....When not supported by someone upon whom you are dependent, document the impact and appeal to other stakeholders to collaborate in pursing a solution. p. 27

MORALE.....If there is low morale in your area, the reason is you. Do something. p.28

TURNOVER.....If turnover is high, the reason is you. Do something. People don't give the real reasons for leaving. Have someone do exit interviews to discover root causes. p. 29

DOING NOTHING.....Got a problem? Do something, even if it is wrong. At least you have a chance at making it better. Doing nothing is a guaranteed bad outcome. p. 32

BLIND HERD MENTALITY.....Train employees to never operate from the position that "we've always done it that way" or "someone told me to do it that way" and to vigorously report problems. p. 33

MASS PUNISHMENT.....Narrow the scope of punishment to the violators. Don't punish everyone for the errs of a few. p. 33

BASHING.....Be a stand up leader and defuse mob behavior. Bring the focus back to business issues and moving forward. p. 36

STYLE.....Find your leadership style. Express it, but do so within the framework of good judgement and company culture. p. 36

Index of Best Practices

BALANCE.....Everything you do to become successful is a matter of balance. You can do too much or too little of anything. p. 37

IMAGE.....Follow the dress code. Dress like the people who make promotion decisions. Keep your work clothes in a separate place in your closet and wear only those to work. p. 37

FIRING.....Have the courage to de-hire. Learn why, when and how to do it right. p. 40

PROMOTING.....Consider the message you are sending when making a promotion decision. Promote based on performance, not seniority. Don't confuse likability with competence. p. 44

INNATE ABILITIES.....Hire people with the innate qualities that match the job. You can give employees knowledge, you cannot give them inherent qualities. p. 44

CAREER PATHS.....Don't promote based only on performance at the current level. Consider whether talents match the new job. Create career paths for high-performing employees. p. 45

HIRING.....Improve the odds of new employee success. Develop highly sophisticated pre-employment screening techniques. p. 45

COST CUTTING.....When laying off, keep the strong performers. Don't apply indiscriminate across-the-board cuts as they may disproportionately increase other costs or reduce revenue. Consider the overall impact of each cost cut. p. 46

OVERWHELMED.....When confronted with projects or promotions for which you think you are not ready, get ready. p. 47

WAVERING.....If you get information that causes you to re-think your position, don't be afraid to change your mind, and don't apologize for it. p. 47

Index of Best Practices

PILOT PROJECTS.....Let people try out their ideas in a controlled, limited environment. p. 51

DIVERSITY.....Create opportunities for interaction between diverse employees. Schedule ethnic lunches and use holiday celebrations of diverse groups as opportunities to educate. p. 51

EXPONENTIAL SYNERGY.....To realize an increasing rate of progress and outcomes superior to individual effort, create strong, productive teams, remove barriers, and invest in learning. p. 54

PROGRESS SQUARED.....Enhance the energy of *exponential synergy* by keeping the momentum going and flowing it to a broader employee base. p. 55

THE WIN.....Avoid the victim mentality. Go for the win. Play the cards you are dealt and win no matter what the challenge. p. 57

VICTIM MENTALITY.....Don't lead your team down the victim path. Respond to every challenge as an opportunity to win and demonstrate what the team can do. p. 57

NUISANCE PROBLEMS.....Use nuisance problems as a mechanism to train staff on project management. Every leader should have an assigned project at all times. p. 59

CALL TO ACTION....Follow every appeal to employees with a specific action request that communicates exactly what you need each person to do individually. p. 60

TAKE THE POWER.....Don't wait for someone to assign you a problem or task. Unless something is specifically prohibited, if in your judgement it needs to be done, do it. p. 60

Index of Best Practices

NURTURING.....Nurture everyone--your employees, your boss, your peers, your associates, and your customers. p. 63

LITTLE THINGS COUNT.....Wear colorful clothes on rainy days. Hang in the parking lot to scrape car widows for employees on snow days. p. 64

GRACE PERIODS.....Soften the impact of change for employees by giving them time to adjust before publishing their performance results. Allow them to "lean into it." p. 64

MENTORING.....Be cautious about formally mentoring unless there is a formal mentoring program in your organization. p. 65

FOLLOWING.....Be a good follower. Routinely provide status reports to your boss whether he requires them or not. Seek his input regularly. Speak your mind but maintain a respectful level of deference. p. 66

PRIORITIES.....Put actions affecting people, removal of barriers, super processes, and releasing exponential synergy on your daily "To Do" list. Do people things during the day and paperwork on off hours. p. 67

PEOPLE FIRST.....Get to work before everyone else for uninterrupted time to organize your day and work your desk so you are free to do people things when employees show up. p. 68

FOCUS.....Don't let the job you want distract you from the job you've got. p. 69

GOAL TRANSLATION.....Collaborate with employees to determine exactly how each individual will contribute toward a goal while doing his job every day. p. 69

Index of Best Practices

CONTEXT.....Put work into context for employees assuring there is an awareness of purpose, vision, mission, plans, goals, strategies, tactics, and values. p. 71

PEOPLE FACTOR.....When selling a sense of purpose to employees, tie their work to how it affects people. Paint a picture by telling stories that illustrate people impact. p. 73

MISSION STATEMENTS.....Have a crisp mission statement for every department and a measurable goal tied to that mission. All employees should be able to state their department's mission and goal as well as their role in accomplishing them. p. 74

PEOPLE PLANNING.....Assess the people component of change and include action steps in project plans to address the people impact. Make people projects a priority on your "To Do" list. p. 77

KEY PLAYERS.....Tell your top people they are key players. They may not know. Ask your staff to do the same. p. 78

FRAME IT UP.....When forming project teams, frame up the project and set the context of the activity up front. Periodically remind team members of the team's purpose. p. 79

FEEDBACK.....Don't be afraid of Q&A. You won't have all the answers, but you sure want to know what all the questions are. Solicit feedback at the end of every communication. p. 80

COMMUNICATION.....Schedule routine communication events like staff meetings, newsletters, weekly reports and town hall meetings. Use *stand up meetings* and *credible messengers* (peer leaders) to disseminate information and provide feedback. p. 80

ELEVATOR SPEECHES.....Every morning on your commute to work consider what issues employees have on their minds and

Index of Best Practices

develop a one or two sentence comment on the topic. Have your leadership team do the same. p. 81

APPRECIATION.....Be constantly vigilant for employees doing a good job and thank them. Say "I appreciate **you**," not "I appreciate **it**." Tell their boss how exceptional they are. Visit work group meetings and thank the team members for their efforts. p. 82

HOOPLA.....Do fun, playful, "big deal" recognition events. p. 82

PERFECTION.....In your quest for perfection, be prepared to settle for the best solution you can get. It may not be perfect. p. 85

STRONG PERFORMERS.....Make decisions that support and reward your best employees. Be careful not to react to poor performers' issues at the cost of the strong ones. p. 87

FAIRNESS.....In general, make decisions that benefit stakeholders in this order: customers first, then the company, the employee base as a whole, and your department. p. 88

FAIRNESS AWARENESS.....Educate all employees on the fact that fairness is in the eye of the beholder. Create awareness of the criteria for decisions. p. 88

REJECTION.....When you advise an employee they did not get a job, tell them that how they handle that news affects their prospects the next time around. Help them become more competitive. p. 89

ADVERSITY.....Take advantage of challenges. Use them to build team cohesiveness and stimulate employees to win, no matter what. p. 91

WORST-CASE SCENARIO.....Help employees cope by considering the worst outcome and how to deal with that, then focus them on more likely scenarios. p. 92

Index of Best Practices

EMOTIONAL INTELLIGENCE.....Study EI and share that learning with your staff. Research opportunities to improve EI in employees. p. 93

DEFENDING EMPLOYEES.....Don't defend indefensible behavior. Remember, when you ignore bad behavior, you endorse it. Hold employees accountable but support them in salvaging the situation and redeeming themselves. p. 95

EXTERNALIZATION.....Don't let employees blame someone else for something for which they are accountable. Call out anyone who throws up decoys. p. 96

REPORTING MISTAKES.....Include requirements for reporting in employee training so they know the consequences for hiding a mistake are more severe than those for the mistake itself. p. 97

THE ROAD TO CONSENSUS.....Train all employees on conflict resolution and consensus building. p. 100

SILO EFFECT.....Be prepared to sacrifice for the good of the whole. When the sacrifice is too great, disclose and discuss, but don't block. p. 101

PROPOSAL FORMATS.....Develop criteria for submitting proposals for approval. Include alternatives, pros and cons, stakeholder perspectives, and dissenting opinions. p.102

WORK MEASUREMENT.....Measure production and quality and give strong performers the recognition they deserve. p. 105

FREE ENTERPRISE AND COMPETITION.....Create awareness among employees of how the free enterprise system works, the nature of competition, and how their performance

Index of Best Practices

impacts the company's ability to thrive and survive in that environment. p. 107

BUDGET AWARENESS.....Educate all employees on the realities of budget constraints and the role costs play in keeping product prices down so their company can compete effectively in the market place. p. 107

PRODUCTIVITY vs QUALITY.....Ensure that employees understand productivity increases do not necessarily mean a reduction in quality. p. 109

PRODUCTIVITY INITIATIVES.....Put the *super process* of improving productivity at the top of your agenda each day and in your strategic plan. p. 111

TRUTH.....When dealing with behaviors, recognize that you cannot always get to the truth. Deal with facts and focus on the business issues and outcomes. p. 113

MANAGING UP.....Interact with peers, teams and the people doing the work. Don't limit yourself to influencing superiors. If someone approaches you for a decision in a vacuum, send them back to get the perspective of all stakeholders. p. 119

THE ENFORCERS.....Include internal enforcers on project teams, in training sessions and planning processes. Tap into internal and external enforcers to ensure compliance with requirements. p.123

ASPIRATION.....People rarely achieve things they don't set out to do. Determine what it takes to get what you want (within the bounds of integrity, of course) and do those things. p. 129

PLATEAUED EMPLOYEES.....Find ways to demonstrate you appreciate and value plateaued employees. p. 130

Index of Best Practices

ENDURANCE.....When times are tough, don't take your marbles and go home. Apply coping strategies and endure. p.135

CHILLING.....Apply chilling as a *coping strategy* in order to endure when things are so bad that you feel like quitting your job. Quit in your mind but go to work every day. p. 136

THIS TOO SHALL PASS.....Apply this *coping strategy* to endure when a mandated program is not working. p.137

PRINCIPLES.....Weigh carefully the prospect of quitting for the principle of the thing. Few principles are worth quitting for. You can't be a change agent if you quit. Endure. p. 139

NON-THREATENING.....Don't broadcast successes or cheerlead too much about your staff. Let outcomes speak for themselves. Exude quiet confidence. Your boss can do the broadcasting. p. 141

CHALLENGING PROJECTS.....Identify a project no one else has the courage to embrace and take it on. Make certain it plays to your strengths. p. 143

HIRING LEADERS.....After the job interview, take the top candidates to lunch before making a job offer. p. 144

LOFTY GOALS.....Determine what you want to accomplish, set lofty goals and then back them up with tactical actions to accomplish them. p. 145

SUPER PROCESSES.....Identify the super processes in your company that influence key success indicators and make improving those processes a high priority. p. 145

INDISPENSABLE EMPLOYEES.....Don't have any. Don't be one. p. 147

Index of Best Practices

DEPTH OF KNOWLEDGE.....Require that knowledge be redundant, and no one is indispensable, including yourself. p. 147

SUCCESSION PLANNING.....Develop employees to ensure you have an adequate depth of human resources to fill any future vacancies. p. 147

CHANGE AGENT.....Embrace fresh ideas. Brainstorm and experiment. Conduct pilot programs. Challenge customs. p. 148

POWER BROKER.....Be the guy who removes barriers, forms liaisons with people of influence, and who connects people with each other. p. 148

OWN IT.....Run your department like you own it, and you need the profits to support your family. p. 149

LEARNING ENVIRONMENT.....Put employee learning at the top of your agenda. Be hands on. Implement programs where everyone is learning and sharing what they learn. Produce a field of experts. p. 151

EXPERT STATUS.....Become an expert on your industry and on basic business principles. Pass what you learn on so your staff knows everything you know. p. 152

SHARING THE LEARNING.....Have a meeting monthly for staff to exchange information on what they have learned. Set a goal that everyone knows what you know. p. 152

TRAINING.....Personally conduct training classes and require your leadership team do the same. p. 155

PERSONAL DEVELOPMENT PLANS.....Have a learning plan for every employee every year. p. 155

Index of Best Practices

IN-HOUSE CURRICULUM.....Have an in-house curriculum of courses to support employee personal development plans. p. 156

BUDDY UP.....To ensure networking and sharing of knowledge, match up two supervisors or managers and have them go to lunch together once a week for a month or two and then rotate. p.157

EMPLOYEE STRENGTHS.....Focus learning as much as possible on developing strengths as opposed to weaknesses. p. 157

EMPLOYEE LOYALTY.....This is a key success indicator and a pervasive factor in the health of a company. Improve it, and you influence many other success indicators. p. 158

INDUSTRY EXPERT.....Become an expert in your industry. Take 30 minutes a day to read industry materials. Become involved in professional groups and join industry organizations. p. 159

BUSINESS FUNDAMENTALS.....Study accounting, finance, economics, statistics, and business law. Pass knowledge on to your staff, relating it to real business situations. p. 160

PUBLIC SPEAKING.....Cultivate speaking and presentation skills and require that your staff do the same. Form an in-house speaking club to review and polish real presentations. p. 162

WRITING SKILLS.....Become an expert on writing proposals, correspondence, and other business documents. Provide opportunities for staff to learn to do the same. p. 162

PERSPECTIVE CHECK.....Before publishing a document, read it from the perspective of all the people who will be reading it and re-write. p. 163

Index of Best Practices

PROJECT PROCESS DOCUMENT.....Have employees generate a document on the requirements for conducting a project, a guide for both leaders and team members. p. 163

STRATEGIC PLANNING.....Develop a plan every year for your department whether it is required or not. Include key people in the process. Broadly communicate the plan. p. 164

CRITICAL THINKING.....Seek information on approaches to rational thought and logic-based decision making. Read a book on critical thinking. p. 165

CLEAR THE MIND.....Exercise when you become so immersed in what you are doing that your brain gets sluggish. Walk on breaks and lunch hours to get the creative juices flowing. p. 165

SAVVY LEADER.....Be the leader who can look back and know he built his base on integrity, valued and talent of others, made a difference, and stood out for all the right reasons. Be the leader who nurtured everyone--those he lead and those he followed. Be the one who in retrospect knows things were better for others because he was there, that he mattered, and he *served*. Be that leader. p. 167

ABOUT THE AUTHOR

Nikki Hanna has a BS Degree in Business Education and Journalism and a Masters in Business Administration. A retired Certified Public Accountant and Toastmaster, she has many years of experience at various levels of management in the business community. She has played key roles in merger and acquisition ventures, been a consultant for national industry task forces, and served on the board of directors for numerous corporate and charity organizations.

While working her way into the senior executive ranks of corporate America, Nikki gained extensive experience at all levels of business organizations and developed proven strategies for effective leadership in immensely divergent business environments. Her experience in dynamic, highly-regulated, manpower-intensive production operations has given her rare insight into effective leadership practices and perspectives.

Now an author and lecturer, Nikki has dedicated herself to enlightening aspiring leaders. In the education arena she lectures at colleges and universities on business and journalism topics and has served as an advisor on curriculum development and strategic planning.

Even the most seasoned leaders will benefit from Nikki's fresh insights, unique perspectives and powerful strategies for becoming savvy leaders. She provides a remarkable wealth of information on creative tactics and best practices targeted at giving the aspiring leader an edge and an organization a wealth of exuberant, profoundly effective leaders. Her focus on building employee loyalty and using leadership as a medium to serve and to make a difference suggests a sense of purpose that encourages leaders to nurture others. The resulting positive influences contribute to a leadership style reflective of inner strength, confidence and integrity and a company rich in flourishing human resources.

Nikki offers seminars, lectures, and coaching on leadership, management, supervision, and team building which will enlighten and energize any work force.

(www.nikkihanna.com)

TO ORDER

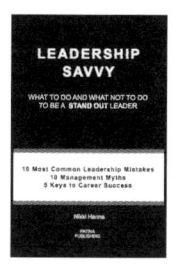

AUTHOR: Nikki Hanna

NAME _____

ADDRESS _____

CITY _____ STATE _____ ZIP _____

PHONE _____ EMAIL _____

Quantity _____ *Leadership Savvy*

Send $19.95 each to:

Patina Publishing
727 S. Norfolk Avenue
Tulsa, Oklahoma 74120

To Order by Phone: 918-587-2451
EMAIL: neqhanna@sbcglobal.net

Order On Line: www.nikkihanna.com

Author is available for presentations and seminars.
A program on *Supervisor Savvy* is also available.
(Visit web site for other books and programs.)